FRESH EGGS DON'T FLOAT

FRESH
Eggs
DON'T FLOAT

*And other tips to help you be
more fearless in the kitchen*

LARA DEPETRILLO AND
CAROLINE EASTMAN-BRIDGES

PIATKUS

PIATKUS

First published in Great Britain in 2008 by Piatkus Books
Copyright © 2008 Lara DePetrillo and Caroline Eastman-Bridges
The moral right of the authors has been asserted

A CIP catalogue record for this book is available from the British Library

ISBN 978-0-7499-0968-0

Designed and typeset in Adobe Garamond by Paul Saunders
Illustations by Raquel Leis Allion
Diagrams by Caroline Eastman-Bridges and Rodney Paull
Printed and bound in Great Britain by
CPI Mackays, Chatham, ME5 8TD

Papers used by Piatkus Books are natural, renewable and recyclable
products made from wood grown in sustainable forests and certified
in accordance with the rules of the Forest Stewardship Council.

Mixed Sources
Product group from well-managed
forests and other controlled sources
www.fsc.org Cert no. SGS-COC-004081
© 1996 Forest Stewardship Council
FSC

Piatkus Books
An imprint of
Little, Brown Book Group
100 Victoria Embankment
London EC4Y 0DY

An Hachette Livre UK Company
www.hachettelivre.co.uk

www.piatkus.co.uk

Contents

Acknowledgements

Lara

Thank you to Albert, the most amazing husband in the world, without whom I never could have written this book. Without you I couldn't do any of the things I do. I love you.

To my beautiful sons, Matthew and Nathaniel for inspiring me to learn how to feed us better. They are my toughest critics, as anyone who is familiar with the honesty of a three- and four-year-old can attest. They are awesome. They fill me with awe. I love you guys.

To all three of them for encouraging my cooking, sharing in my triumphs, and suffering through my failures.

Thank you to Carrie for being my friend, my fellow cooking enthusiast and my writing partner.

Thank you to all my family and friends for all the support.

Caroline

Thank you to my wonderfully hungry family who are always willing test subjects and cheerleaders. Thanks especially to my husband whose complete support and love make all my endeavours possible. To my sister Bronwen for her steadfast intolerance of b******t. To Dad for all his great advice. To Lara, one of my oldest and dearest friends who threw herself into this project without ever looking back. And of course, my Mom who always has the right answer.

Introduction

·

How This All Began

Everyone knows the difference between a flirtation and a serious relationship: at some point flirtation stops and some kind of commitment begins. Cooking is absolutely like that.

DELIA SMITH

Caroline

The creative mind plays with the objects it loves – so says Carl Jung – and I love food. I love the invention, the immediate gratification, the fact that so many ingredients are more readily available now than ever before. I love that I am what I eat. I love how much you can learn about a culture or a person by the kind of food they prepare. Most of all, I like to cook. I keep an open mind and palate and try always to push the boundaries forward.

A few years ago I started to make a list of every ingredient, dish, technique, type of cooking and food I had heard about and wanted to try, or about which I knew nothing other than the name and thought it warranted investigation. I needed a project. I had two small children and had to cook for my family and the list prompted me to decide to make a different dish every day for a year. Some recipes led me down the rabbit hole like *Alice in Wonderland* and gave me a new way of looking at particular types of food or at the culture they came from. My search for ingredients took me to strange and wonderful parts of the places I lived, where the grocery shops smelt like another country. Every shopping trip became a mini vacation. Every dish and technique gave me a better understanding of how to use the ingredients I had searched out. I blogged it all at http://cookbad.blogspot.com from the great successes to the ridiculous disasters. Halfway through the year I invited Lara to join the project and the blog. We were both on a mission together.

Lara

I grew up in New York City where you can get any kind of food you want from anywhere in the world, so I've always had a deep love for a wide variety of food, but I found cooking intimidating. I had a recipe or two that I felt comfortable with, but not much more. When I got pregnant, and especially when my kids were born, the importance of good nutrition became stunningly obvious. I started reading everything about food I could get my hands on. Unfortunately this led to my feeling even more overwhelmed and under qualified to produce nutritious food. Then one day I realised a simple truth: I just needed to start cooking. If you cook the food yourself and use quality ingredients, you will eat well. After that I was off: I learnt how to make the dishes from my childhood I never see any more; the meals from my favourite restaurants I can't get to as often as I'd like with two small children at home; anything that I loved to eat; anything I'd always wanted to try. I was hooked, I loved it. That's when Caroline invited me to join the challenge of cooking a new dish every day for a year and to participate in the food blog.

Keeping the blog was a great way to see the progress I had made and, as I added more and more things to it, I often thought how great it would be to have all the tips together in one place to refer to when I needed to. And that's why we took the next logical step and got together to write this book.

Caroline and Lara

The blog has allowed us to share recipes, learn from and encourage each other to be more creative. It has also been a way to keep in touch, by sharing something we both feel so passionate about. The initial year has long since passed but we continue, unable to stop because food has become our artistic medium of choice.

We learnt a great deal over the course of our challenge – different techniques, shortcuts, substitutions – but the most important things were usually the most basic. For example, if you want to try making something, just do it. It will usually work, and every success will make you more confident, which will make the next challenge easier. Or this: prepare well; do all your chopping and measuring in advance. The last thing you want is for the onions to start burning when you haven't begun to chop the carrots or to find that you don't actually have a key ingredient.

And, finally, this: stay calm. A chef once told me that if you start with good ingredients, it's hard to make a mistake that can't be rectified. With some advance planning, some lists, some practice and a calming mantra (one thing at a time and everything will get done, one thing at a time ...) you'll find there is nothing you can't cook yourself.

That's what we hope this book can do for you.

Chapter one

·

Stuff You Need

I don't like gourmet cooking or 'this' cooking or 'that' cooking. I like good cooking.

JAMES BEARD, American chef and food writer (1903–85)

Equipment

Before we started the cooking challenge our kitchens were full of stuff. Some of it was entirely useless, some of it was essential but completely buried, and some necessities were entirely missing. Over the course of the year we got rid of some old things, got new things, and sometimes bought new things only to get rid of them. In the end we had a much better understanding of what made our cooking life easier. Every cook has his or her own list of necessities, it has a lot to do with the type of cooking you enjoy, whether it's baking, stir frying or hosting dinner parties, but whatever type of cooking you do, the following list is a good jumping-off point. To begin with, if you think you have too much useless kitchen stuff, toss out anything you haven't used in two years.

Essentials

Utensils

- knives: paring, butcher, slicing and bread – all professionally sharpened annually
- spatulas: metal or plastic (for flipping and lifting), wooden, silicone (for scraping bowls)
- spoons: wooden, slotted, measuring
- tongs: rubber tipped if you use non-stick pots and pans
- vegetable peeler
- whisk
- can opener/bottle opener
- corkscrew

Cookware and bakeware

- saucepans: a 1 litre, 2–3 litre and a great big lidded one
- frying pans: heavy bottomed, small, medium and large, all with lids
- medium-sized roasting tin or shallow casserole dish
- lidded cast-iron casserole dish
- tins: muffin, loaf

- baking sheet: don't mess with the cheap ones; get to a restaurant supply shop and get two of the largest that will fit the oven

Gadgets

- electric beater
- kitchen timer, even if the oven has one, another is useful to have around

Other necessities

- metal bowl – good for making a double boiler
- two plastic mixing bowls – one large, one small
- box grater
- measuring jug for liquid
- accurate scales
- wire-mesh strainer
- medium-sized funnel
- colander
- rolling pin
- cotton or linen kitchen towels
- oven gloves
- clingfilm
- baking/parchment paper
- foil

Just to give you an idea of how one kitchen might differ from another, here are some personal choices from each of us. Caroline finds these things indispensable:

- cast-iron pan

- set of nesting bowls

- standing mixer

- sugar thermometer

Lara couldn't live without these:

- springform cake tin

- long-handled fork

- steamer: metal or bamboo

- food processor

Nice to have

Utensils

- pastry brush (get the silicone kind, they work just as well, are easier to clean and last longer)

- 20cm-long knife for carving

- meat mallet

- baster

- roasting rack

- zester

Cookware and bakeware

- non-stick pan – you may want all your pans to be non stick (remember: never use metal utensils on them – they'll ruin the surface)
- ramekins with lids
- soufflé dishes
- baking beans
- pizza stone
- cast-iron griddle

Gadgets

- hand-held blender
- electric steamer
- juicer
- standing mixer with dough hook and paddle attachment

Other things that are nice to have

- hand juicer
- salad spinner
- knife block
- nutcracker
- meat cleaver

Choosing saucepans

Ideally choose a pan without plastic-coated handles so it can go from hob to oven. If you can get your hands on one of these, snap it up because you'll find it incredibly useful. Here are a few tips:

- Copper evenly distributes heat, retains heat, doesn't discolour food and is beautiful. It's also expensive, needs to be polished and, after much use, needs to be resurfaced.

- Aluminium retains heat, heats evenly, but might discolour your food.

- Stainless steel stays shiny, doesn't discolour food but can create hot spots and not cook food evenly.

- Cast iron: when well seasoned performs like non stick. It retains heat, and heats evenly.

  - Cast-iron bonus: if you don't get enough iron in your diet, cooking in a cast-iron pan will introduce iron into any food cooked in it, upping your intake.

  - Cleaning cast iron involves simply wiping it clean or using salt as an abrasive to clean harder to remove bits. Heating it briefly after cleaning to remove leftover moisture will keep it from rusting.

- To stick or not to stick?

Pros	**Cons**
non-stick technology has improved hugely	cannot use with metal utensils
non-stick coatings now last longer	doesn't caramelise food
easy to clean	
harder to get burnt bits in your food	
less troublesome egg cooking	

Alternatives for tools you may not have

- standing mixer: your hands, an electric beater or whisk
- meat mallet: rolling pin or the back of a spoon or a hammer
- blenders and food processors are often interchangeable
- coffee grinder: spice grinder
- mortar and pestle: a freezer bag and a rolling pin
- double boiler: metal bowl set over a saucepan of water
- sifter: strainer – put flour in and gently shake
- pastry cutter: the back of a fork or a knife
- biscuit cutters: a glass
- zester: fine grater or vegetable peeler if you want strips

Food

'Tell me what you eat,' wrote the nineteenth-century French gastronome Jean-Anthelme Brillat-Savarin, 'and I shall tell you what you are.'

When you have your cupboards and fridge stocked with some basic items, it's really easy to find things to make on the spur of the moment, and it will also be easier to use cookery books. I can't tell you how often I have looked warily at a recipe with a ridiculously long ingredient list, only to find that I only needed to buy one or two things because I already had the rest to hand. The more you cook, the more you'll find your own style, and what you use on a regular basis will become more obvious. Until then, the list below is a great place to start.

Great to have in your pantry

- anchovies, tinned
- baking powder
- bicarbonate of soda
- bread: sandwich, crusty, pitta, wraps, tortilla, crumbs (or make them yourself)
- chocolate chips
- cocoa, unsweetened – the good kind
- coconut milk
- coffee, instant
- corn for popping
- cornflour

- cornmeal
- dried fruit: raisins, currants, etc.
- flour: unbleached, all purpose
- honey
- horseradish
- hot sauce
- jam or preserves
- ketchup
- mayonnaise
- mushrooms, dried
- nuts: almonds, peanuts, walnuts, pine nuts
- oatmeal
- oil: olive, vegetable, sesame
- pastas
- peanut or other nut butter
- potatoes
- pulses: tinned and dried
- rice
- salt
- sherry
- soy sauce

- stock: good quality
- sugar: white, brown, icing, caster
- tomato purée
- tomatoes, tinned: whole and chopped
- tuna or salmon, tinned
- vanilla extract: the good kind
- vinegars: balsamic, white wine, red wine, rice and apple cider
- Worcestershire sauce
- yeast, instant

Nice to have around

- dry vermouth
- fish sauce
- Grand Marnier or its cheaper second cousin, triple sec
- pickles: gherkins, pickled onions, etc.
- red wine
- desiccated coconut
- soba (buckwheat) noodles

Great to have in the fridge

- bacon

- brown sauce

- butter

- cabbage

- capers

- carrots

- celery

- cheeses

- cucumbers

- double cream

- eggs

- fats: bacon, butter, duck fat, margarine

- garlic

- golden syrup

- green vegetables

- herbs, fresh: thyme, mint, basil, coriander, chives

- leeks

- lemons, limes or their respective juices

- milk: whole, semi-skimmed fresh or soya

- mustard: Dijon, grain, English

- olives
- onions
- peppers
- spring onions
- yoghurt

Nice to have around

- maple syrup
- pesto
- sweet chilli dipping sauce
- tofu

Great to have in the freezer

- berries
- bread – crusty
- chicken breast
- corn on the cob
- home-made stock – and bits and scraps to be made into stock
- ice cream
- pastry: puff, filo
- peas, green beans, lima beans, edamame (soya beans)
- sausages

A *basic spice list*

- basil
- bay leaves
- black peppercorns
- cayenne pepper
- chillies, powdered, crushed
- cinnamon, ground and sticks
- cumin, ground
- curry powder
- mustard, powdered
- nutmeg, ground and whole
- oregano
- paprika
- parsley
- rosemary
- sage
- thyme

Trinity, triad or holy trinity

The aromatics (usually three, sometimes more) that make up the flavour base of a regional cuisine. The term was originally coined to refer to bell peppers, celery and onions – the basis of Cajun cooking. Here are the aromatics for the following countries:

China	garlic, ginger, spring onion, Chinese five-spice powder: cinnamon, cloves, fennel, Szechuan pepper, star anise
France	fines herbes: chervil, chives, parsley, tarragon mirepoix: 2 parts onion, 1 part celery, 1 part carrots
India	ginger, onion, garlic
Italy	garlic, onion, tomato *bagna cauda* (hot bath): a sauce of olive oil, butter, anchovies, lemon zest
Mexico	corn, beans, chilli peppers
Middle East	garlic, lemon, olive oil
Spain	garlic, onion and tomato cooked in olive oil
Szechwan	garlic, ginger, chilli
Thailand	galangal, kaffir lime leaf, lemongrass.

Chapter two

·

Stocks and Sauces

A well-made sauce will make even an elephant or a
grandfather palatable.

GRIMOD DE LA REYNIÈRE, French chef and food writer (1758–1837)

I n many households, making a sauce means opening a jar.
This may seem an easy solution, but the fact is there are
many pasta sauces that can be made in the time it takes to
boil the water and cook the pasta. Once you get the basics of
sauce construction, you can turn just about anything in the
fridge into a resplendent meal.

Definitions

Bouquet garni (pronounced boo-KAY gahr-NEE) A little herb
bouquet generally made with parsley, a bay leaf, a few sprigs
of thyme and some celery or celery leaves (there are many

variations) that is thrown into a stock or sauce. The herbs are either tied together with string or placed in a cheesecloth pouch for easy removal after cooking. They can be bought ready made in the spice section of most supermarkets.

Caramelising Cooking slowly over a low heat, past the point where the food is cooked, until the natural (or added) sugars turn brown.

Deglazing Making a quick sauce by adding liquid to a pan that has been used to cook meat, poultry or fish. Simmer gently for a few minutes or sometimes just seconds to incorporate any juices or crunchy bits from the pan.

Emulsifying Combining two liquids together that normally don't mix easily, like oil and water.

Breaking Failed emulsifying. When a sauce in the process of emulsifying, stops doing so, it separates and breaks apart. This can be caused by several things, and can occur at any point in the process, even after the sauce is finished.

Mirepoix (pronounced mir-pwa) A combination of 2 parts onion, 1 part carrot, 1 part celery, diced.

To sweat Sautéing a mirepoix or other vegetable, just long enough to soften, without browning or caramelising.

Taking stock

Stock is made from vegetables, herbs and spices (with or without meat, poultry or fish) simmered in water for a long time to coax out the flavour of the ingredients into the water. It can be used as a base for soups, sauces or stews or as a replacement for water to make a dish more flavourful.

Devoted cooks have stockpots going pretty much constantly on their stove tops. They throw in any appropriate leftover vegetables and meat and scoop stock out of the pot, strain it and use it as needed. For stock, the mantra is: always skim, always strain.

Three basic stocks

Stock tip number 1

Avoid any vegetables that colour the stock – tomatoes, for example.

Light stock

1. Toss the washed raw bones from 1 or 2 chicken carcasses (if you are a herbivore, skip the chicken and just work with vegetables; great stocks can be meat free), including necks, gizzards, giblets, wings into a large pot and add any or all of the following: carrots, onions, garlic, celery, parsley, parsnips, fennel, rosemary, mushrooms, bay leaf, thyme, whole peppercorns, leeks. Never use broccoli, cabbage or cauliflowers because their flavours will overpower the stock. Salt only very lightly and correct the seasoning when the stock is finished.

2. Cover the stock makings with cold water and then add a little more. Cold water is good because the more time it takes the stock to come to a boil, the longer the water has to draw out the blood and other undesirable organic matter from the bones before the heat of the water seals

them. All that stuff will rise to the top of your stock looking like foam or scum and should be skimmed off.

3. Simmer covered – don't boil, for between 3 to 8 hours.

4. Skim any foam off the top.

5. Strain the heck out of it. Strain more times that you think is necessary. Ideally you would use a chinois – a very fine conical-shaped strainer that allows you to mash down the stock ingredients and get out every last bit of liquid, but any strainer will do, as will putting some cheesecloth in the bottom of a colander. After straining, skim off all excess fat.

Stock tip number 2

In the spirit of wasting as little food as possible, collect onion skins, garlic tips and skins, celery bottoms, unused portions of carrots, mushroom trimmings, fennel cores and any bones, raw or cooked. Keep them in a bag in the fridge or freezer for when it's stock time. Any herbs that you have been saving in the freezer and may be at the end of their run are also good candidates.

Dark stock

> ### Stock tip number 3
>
> Rub the bones with a little tomato purée, and sprinkle with some flour before roasting for extra flavour and thickness.

This stock is made from roasted veal bones and can be used for sauces or soups. Beef bones can be used as a substitute, but they will make an overpoweringly beef-flavoured stock. Veal is more subtle. Although the entire process takes about 12 hours it isn't labour intensive, it's quite easy.

1. Get 2.5 kilos of veal bones. Preheat the oven to 180°C/gas mark 4.

2. Wash and dry the bones and roast for 1 to 2 hours until well browned, but not black or burnt.

3. While the bones are roasting make a mirepoix weighing about 700g, chop the vegetables and roast them.

4. Put the bones in a large saucepan with the mirepoix, some peppercorns, bay, thyme and salt. There will be lots of rendered fat left over from the bones on the baking sheet. Don't add that to the stock. Cover the bones and mirepoix with cold water and simmer – not boil – for between 8 and 10 hours. Then strain, strain, strain and skim off all the fat.

To make shop-bought stock taste better, put it on the stove and add any of the following:
onions, carrots, celery, wine (white for chicken or vegetables, red for beef), parsley, bay leaf, thyme and leftover poultry or meat. Boil for about 1 to 2 hours, then strain.

Fish stock or fumet

1. Collect the racks (the spine and bones) of several non-oily fish. Fish heads with eyes and gills removed are good if you have some around, and so are prawn, lobster or crab shells that have been lightly roasted (prawn shells roast very quickly) and any of the vegetables, herbs and spices from the light stock recipe above.

2. Cover everything with cold water and then add a bit more. Simmering for 30 to 40 minutes is sufficient, and in some cases, cooking longer can actually ruin the stock. Unless your recipe specifies longer cooking, stick with half an hour.

3. See step 4 and 5 from light stock.

4. You can add some lemon during the final seasoning correction.

Stock tip number 4

The addition of clam juice to chicken stock is a shortcut to fumet in fast recipes.

Sauce

A sauce is generally made of four parts: flavour base + liquid + thickener + seasoning. Julia Child (the chef who introduced French cooking to America) says, 'A sauce should not be considered a disguise or mask; its role is to point up, to prolong, or to compliment the tastes of the food it accompanies, or to contrast with it, or to give variety to its mode of presentation.'

Step 1: flavour base

This consists of aromatic vegetables, herbs or spices cooked in fat to release their flavour. When you add whatever liquid you are using, it will take on all these flavours.

Step 2: the liquids

Loads of options here: stock, wine, brandy, cider, beer, milk, cream, butter, yoghurt, crème fraîche, fruit juice, coconut milk, vegetable purée.

Step 3: thickeners

Most of the sauces in this chapter use a roux as the thickener. Roux (pronounced roo) is equal weights of fat and flour cooked together to prepare the flour particles to absorb liquid. They come in shades from white to chocolate, and must be stirred constantly while cooking so they won't burn. Cooking roux for 2 minutes will give you a white roux, the base for many sauces. The longer the roux is cooked the darker it becomes. The darker it gets, the nuttier and richer the flavour is. On the other hand, as it darkens, it has less and less thickening power. Undercooked roux can give a raw floury taste and not thicken properly.

> A very dark roux will have a quarter the thickening power (by weight) of a white roux.

A roux of thumb

For a thin sauce or soup: 1 tablespoon flour and 1 tablespoon butter per 225ml liquid

For a thicker basic sauce: 1½ tablespoons flour and 1½ tablespoons butter per 225ml

You can go up to 2 tablespoons for a really thick sauce. It all comes down to personal preference and making sure it matches the rest of the dish.

Some other thickening options

ARROWROOT

Heat reaction – Thickens at very low heat, good for egg-based sauces
Flavour – Neutral
Characteristics – Only thickens for a few minutes; will not thicken if reheated
Amounts – 10g for 240ml liquid

BLOOD

Heat reaction – Will not thicken if boiled, simmer gently
Flavour – Meaty
Characteristics – Add at the last minute; work very gently
Amounts – Arbitrary

BUTTER

Heat reaction – Add cold to heated sauce, remove pan from heat, swirl until melted
Flavour – Delicious, will always improve the flavour of a sauce
Characteristics – Only use if sauce is being served immediately; creates a lovely glossy finish
Amounts – 15g for 240ml liquid

CORNFLOUR

Heat reaction – Can be boiled with no ill effects
Flavour – Has a flavour that needs to be cooked out
Characteristics – Creates a cloudy finish, so it is best used for milk or opaque sauces; over beating will reduce thickening ability
Amounts – 15g for 240ml liquid

EGG YOLK

Heat reaction – Heat with extreme caution or you will end up with scrambled eggs
Flavour – Custardy
Characteristics – If added very slowly and whisked constantly it will emulsify
Amounts – Arbitrary

KUDZU OR KUZU* (see definition on page 29)

Heat reaction – Easily absorbs hot or cold liquids
Flavour – Neutral
Characteristics – Non-fat, low in calories, binds more strongly than arrowroot
Amounts – 15g for 240ml liquid

LIAISON

Heat reaction – Add just after sauce comes off the heat
Flavour – Adds richness
Characteristics – 2 parts double cream combined with a
beaten egg yolk, gives a creamy texture to velouté
Amounts – 120ml double cream and 1 egg yolk for 2 litres
of sauce

POTATO STARCH

Heat reaction – Do not heat above 176°C or it will start
to thin
Flavour – Neutral
Characteristics – Creates a translucent, glossy sauce, only
thickens for a short time
Amounts – 15ml for 240ml of liquid

REDUCTION

Heat reaction – Reduce at low heat, simmer, don't boil
Flavour – Intensification of flavour, so season after you
reduce
Characteristics – Can end up overly salty if you start with
a salty liquid
Amounts – N/A

ROUX

Heat reaction – Must be stirred constantly while over
heat, changes dramatically in flavour the longer it is
cooked
Flavour – Floury, unless it has been cooked long enough
Characteristics – The darker it gets the less thickening
power it has
Amounts – 1 part butter, 1 part flour

* Kudzu is a Japanese thickener made from the kudzu or kuzu root, which is also said to help cure a hangover or headache.

Some tips from Caroline

Here are a few of the tricks I learnt while experimenting with thickeners:

- Adding a purée of roasted vegetables, garlic or potatoes, will thicken without adding fat and gives a fullness that will enrich your sauce immensely.

- Whipping in breadcrumbs is another low-fat way to thicken sauces. They will thicken very quickly because the starch has already been cooked out.

- Onions can also thicken sauces if you use a huge amount (in curries, for example), as do grated carrots, bananas and peanuts.

- Fruit and vegetables can make good sauces on their own. Make a purée, or just chop some cooked (or raw but naturally soft) fruit or vegetables, then add liquid and reduce to the desired consistency. This is a good way to use the vegetables from the roasting pan to go with the roasted meat.

Step 4: seasoning

The final step in any recipe, whether written or not, is 'adjust seasoning to taste'.

Caroline learned this tip the hard way: when you make a sauce, use a heavy-bottomed pan because it conducts heat evenly and prevents burning. Avoid using aluminium saucepans because they discolour some foods and I have turned many a sauce grey, before I worked out it was the pan and not some gruesome ingredient mistake.

Easy peasy pan sauce and gravy

In its simplest form, gravy is just a thickened mixture of the drippings and beautiful dark caramelised bits that come from the roasting meat or poultry. To make it you:

1. Skim off any extra fat before you start.

2. Deglaze the pan using liquid (stock, wine, beer, cider, can be just about anything).

3. Thicken, usually with cream, roux, potato starch or corn-flour.

For pan sauce, just skip step 3.

That's it! If you want to do more, browning some onions or garlic before you carry on with the deglazing should give you an extra good gravy, even if you are just using a pan that was used for a quickly sautéed piece of meat. As a matter of fact, you could make a gravy or pan sauce without a meat pan, just use the browned onions in fat as a base.

The five mother sauces

The nineteenth-century chef Antonin Carême introduced the idea of the mother sauces, concoctions that were the base of most French sauces. Other then a few modifications made by the chef Escoffier in the early twentieth century, this is still the model used and taught today in French and many other types of cooking. If all the names and pedigrees below make you want to skip them, focus on perfecting pan gravies. Pan gravy is just as good and completely uninterested in making you feel inadequate.

Béchamel or White Sauce

Béchamel is the base for soufflés, the cosy host for macaroni and cheese, often the base for gratins and lasagne as well as many other baked Italian pasta dishes, and a main ingredient of moussaka. It's the kind of thing that, after you've made it a few times, you won't even bother to measure. You will just do it by feel.

FOR 225ml
2 tablespoons butter
3 tablespoons flour
350ml milk
salt and freshly ground pepper

Combine butter and flour (roux) in a saucepan and stir constantly over a medium-high heat for 2 minutes. Then add the milk all at once, and whisk until fully combined. Whisk as the milk simmers for 5 to 12 minutes depending on how thick you want it. Julia Child would have you add the milk hot, in which case it thickens spectacularly – essentially instantly.

Some tips from Lara

- If you are planning on adding cheese, herbs or vegetables, do it a couple of minutes after adding the milk to the roux.

- Sweating some diced onion in the butter before adding the flour, or using milk that has been infused with an onion stuck with a clove gives a savoury flavour to the sauce, as does a pinch of nutmeg to finish.

Velouté

Similar to béchamel, but you use a light stock instead of milk.

FOR 225ml
2 tablespoons butter
2 tablespoons flour
300ml light stock, heated

Combine the butter and flour in a saucepan and cook over a medium heat for 2 minutes, then remove from the heat. When the roux stops bubbling, turn the heat to low and gradually add the stock, stirring continuously until it is combined. Cook for a few minutes to make sure it is not floury tasting. Correct the seasoning.

Traditionally, velouté was supposed to cook for several hours, but if you cook the roux properly and use good-quality stock, you can get the same results without putting in as much time. If you want to go old school, put the sauce into a double boiler and cook very slowly for an hour, stirring often.

This is not one of Caroline's rules, but she would like to mention that with velouté the sauce should match its host, so if you're making a sauce for fish, it should be made with fumet, instead of light stock. Sounds uptight and it is. It's fancy stuff and I have often suspected that it is silently judging me.

Espagnole or Brown Sauce

On its own, espagnole may not seem like much, but if you have some to hand you can make an amazing range of sauces in no time. It's perfect for when you are grilling, to dress up leftovers, or for any time your dinner looks a little plain. Always use really good-quality stock. The flavour of the sauce comes from the stock reduction, so the quality of the stock is going to have a massive influence on the finished sauce. Make sure the stock isn't too salty because the saltiness will intensify as it reduces. Also, be very careful making the roux – don't stop stirring. After 10 minutes it'll feel like 20, but soldier on, the results will be worth it. If the roux burns, it will damage its thickening power and ruin the taste.

FOR 470ml
110g mirepoix
25g butter
25g flour
710ml brown stock, hot
25ml passata
1 bouquet garni

In a saucepan sauté the mirepoix in the butter until well browned. Add the flour and stir to make a roux. Continue to cook for about 15 to 20 minutes until the roux is browned, stirring constantly. Then gradually stir in the brown stock and passata. Keep stirring until the mixture begins to simmer.

Skim the surface. Add the bouquet garni and simmer until the sauce is reduced by ⅔ (this may take an hour or two). Continue to skim. Strain through muslin cloth as many times as you can stand.

· A TIP FROM CAROLINE ·

This sauce takes a while to make, so it's great to make a big batch of it and then divide it into portions and freeze.

Tomato Sauce

Tomato sauce is very diverse. It is needed for everything from our beloved spag bol, to salsa, to ketchup (is there nothing a tomato can't do?) The varieties are endless. From uncooked sauces made with fresh chopped tomatoes and fresh herbs mixed together and tossed into pasta, to thick, rich, cooked sauces just sitting on the stove top all day till they are beautifully reduced and blended. Don't be afraid to experiment with this kind of sauce, there are no hard and fast rules, just about anything works. As an example, here is one of Lara's favourites – the simplest tomato sauce ever: chop some garlic, throw it in a saucepan with some olive oil and cook gently until it has softened a bit. Add a couple of anchovies, press them with a spoon and stir them till they melt (yes, they melt). Throw in a handful of chopped tomatoes, or cherry tomatoes cut in half, and let them heat through. Toss with pasta and eat.

Hollandaise

This is very similar to mayonnaise but uses melted clarified butter instead of oil. Try it. Partly because there's no more glorious substance on earth than fresh hollandaise, partly because it will amaze your friends (and yourself) with its almost magical appearance right there in the pan, and partly because, once you've mastered it, a whole range of other sauces (check out the chart on pages 36–7) just fall in line. Folks will tell you that you will most certainly destroy your first, second . . . third batch. That talk is complete and utter malarkey. Some techniques may make it more prone to breaking, more likely that you will scramble your egg yolks than emulsify them but this recipe is easy – it's unbreakable hollandaise.

FOR 300ml
4 egg yolks
300g butter
salt and pepper
juice of ½–1 lemon

Beat the egg yolks in a bowl until they are pale. Heat the butter in a small saucepan and skim the white foamy stuff off the top. Keep it pretty hot but do not let it bubble. Let the milk solids in the butter sink to the bottom. Keep beating the egg yolks as you very slowly pour a bit of hot butter into them. Let it emulsify, then add some more, then a bit more until the butter is used up. Add salt, pepper and lemon juice, and you're done. Serve immediately. If you can't and you want to keep it hot, put it in a double boiler over a very low heat and stir often.

Derivations of the 5 Mother Sauces

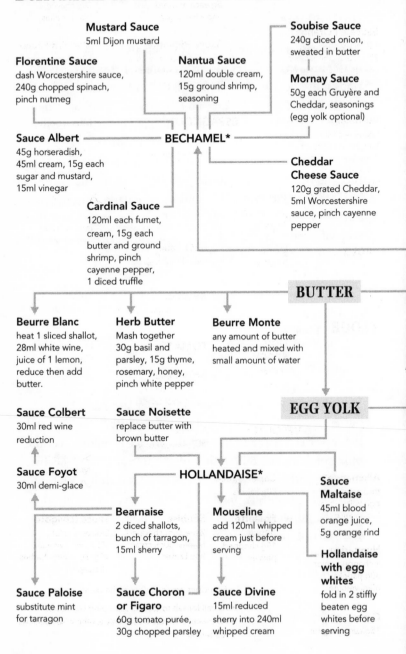

Mustard Sauce
5ml Dijon mustard

Soubise Sauce
240g diced onion,
sweated in butter

Florentine Sauce
dash Worcestershire sauce,
240g chopped spinach,
pinch nutmeg

Nantua Sauce
120ml double cream,
15g ground shrimp,
seasoning

Mornay Sauce
50g each Gruyère and
Cheddar, seasonings
(egg yolk optional)

Sauce Albert
45g horseradish,
45ml cream, 15g each
sugar and mustard,
15ml vinegar

BECHAMEL*

Cheddar Cheese Sauce
120g grated Cheddar,
5ml Worcestershire
sauce, pinch cayenne
pepper

Cardinal Sauce
120ml each fumet,
cream, 15g each
butter and ground
shrimp, pinch
cayenne pepper,
1 diced truffle

BUTTER

Beurre Blanc
heat 1 sliced shallot,
28ml white wine,
juice of 1 lemon,
reduce then add
butter.

Herb Butter
Mash together
30g basil and
parsley, 15g thyme,
rosemary, honey,
pinch white pepper

Beurre Monte
any amount of butter
heated and mixed with
small amount of water

EGG YOLK

Sauce Colbert
30ml red wine
reduction

Sauce Noisette
replace butter with
brown butter

Sauce Foyot
30ml demi-glace

HOLLANDAISE*

Sauce Maltaise
45ml blood
orange juice,
5g orange rind

Bearnaise
2 diced shallots,
bunch of tarragon,
15ml sherry

Mouseline
add 120ml whipped
cream just before
serving

Sauce Paloise
substitute mint
for tarragon

Sauce Choron or Figaro
60g tomato purée,
30g chopped parsley

Sauce Divine
15ml reduced
sherry into 240ml
whipped cream

Hollandaise with egg whites
fold in 2 stiffly
beaten egg
whites before
serving

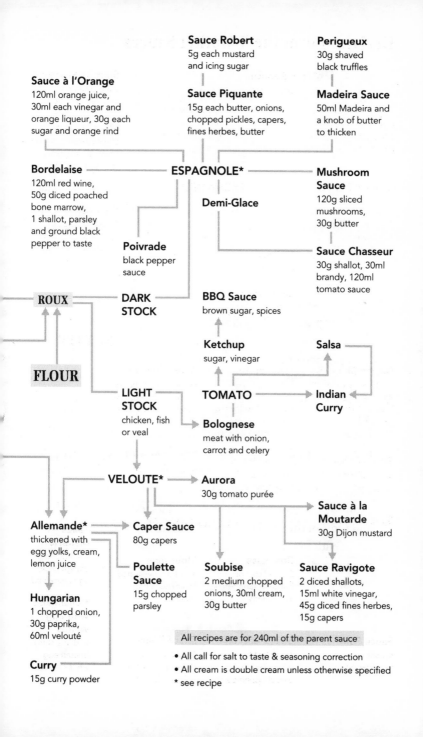

Sauce Robert
5g each mustard and icing sugar

Perigueux
30g shaved black truffles

Sauce à l'Orange
120ml orange juice, 30ml each vinegar and orange liqueur, 30g each sugar and orange rind

Sauce Piquante
15g each butter, onions, chopped pickles, capers, fines herbes, butter

Madeira Sauce
50ml Madeira and a knob of butter to thicken

Bordelaise
120ml red wine, 50g diced poached bone marrow, 1 shallot, parsley and ground black pepper to taste

ESPAGNOLE*

Mushroom Sauce
120g sliced mushrooms, 30g butter

Demi-Glace

Poivrade
black pepper sauce

Sauce Chasseur
30g shallot, 30ml brandy, 120ml tomato sauce

ROUX

DARK STOCK

BBQ Sauce
brown sugar, spices

Ketchup
sugar, vinegar

Salsa

FLOUR

LIGHT STOCK
chicken, fish or veal

TOMATO

Indian Curry

Bolognese
meat with onion, carrot and celery

VELOUTE* → **Aurora**
30g tomato purée

Sauce à la Moutarde
30g Dijon mustard

Allemande*
thickened with egg yolks, cream, lemon juice

Caper Sauce
80g capers

Poulette Sauce
15g chopped parsley

Soubise
2 medium chopped onions, 30ml cream, 30g butter

Sauce Ravigote
2 diced shallots, 15ml white vinegar, 45g diced fines herbes, 15g capers

Hungarian
1 chopped onion, 30g paprika, 60ml velouté

Curry
15g curry powder

All recipes are for 240ml of the parent sauce

- All call for salt to taste & seasoning correction
- All cream is double cream unless otherwise specified
- * see recipe

The best of British
(see? they're not all French!)

Bread Sauce

For this sauce, milk is infused with extra flavours, and then thickened with breadcrumbs and butter. It is most often served with poultry. Recipes for this vary wildly because it all depends on how spiced, how thick and how creamy you like your bread sauce to be. Here's a jumping off point:

FOR ABOUT 500ml
450ml milk
1 onion stuck with 15 cloves
1 bay leaf
5 peppercorns
50–150g breadcrumbs
50g butter

Put the milk in a saucepan with the clove-studded onion, bay leaf and peppercorns. Bring it to a boil and then let it cool down. You can leave it to infuse for much longer (even overnight) if you have the time and the inclination. After straining the milk, warm it back up, and add the breadcrumbs and most of the butter, reserving a small knob of butter to add at the end. Let the sauce thicken, it shouldn't take longer than 15 minutes. Add the remaining butter, mix it in well, and adjust the seasoning just before serving.

Mayonnaise: a Basic Building Block

What's in a name?

Mayonnaise may have originally been called mayhonnaise after Port Mahon on the island of Minorca. Some say the French brought it back from Spain after winning a battle there. Others say the name is derived from the word *moyeu*, a medieval French word for egg yolk that has fallen out of common use. It meant centre or hub.

Beloved though it may be for sandwiches, it is also a sauce in its own right. Making your own will also open up a range of different flavours and variations. A blender, hand mixer, stick blender and standing mixer all work very well for making mayonnaise, but making it by hand, with a whisk, is by all accounts the way to go for the most lovely, glistening, thick mayonnaise. Still, you have to have a very strong arm and mad whisking skills.

FOR ABOUT 450ml

4 egg yolks
½ teaspoon Dijon mustard or ¼ teaspoon dry mustard
350ml extra virgin olive oil
juice of 1 lemon
½–1 teaspoon white wine vinegar
salt and pepper

It's good to have all these ingredients as well as the bowl and whisk at room temperature, but we didn't and it worked out just fine.

Whisk the egg yolks and mustard until they are pale yellow. Put the oil into something that will allow you to pour it very slowly. While the egg yolks are being beaten, slowly pour ½ teaspoon of oil onto them. When it has emulsified add another ½ teaspoon and so on. Towards the end, you can start to pour the oil a bit faster but if you incorporate it too quickly the mayonnaise will break. Add salt, pepper, lemon juice and vinegar.

The first time you make it, try to draw the whole process out to half an hour. The slower you add the oil, the less likely you are to break the mayonnaise.

Caroline's favourite way to make mayonnaise

You can trade the olive oil for other oils or the lemon juice for anything else acidic. The most wonderful mayonnaise I've ever made is one in which the oil is replaced with rendered bacon fat and tomato pulp instead of lemon juice. It's dangerously delicious.

Weather report

According to the *Joy of Cooking*, you should not try to make mayonnaise in a thunderstorm or if there is one on the way. For some reason beyond our imagination it won't bind.

The chart opposite shows all the sauces and dressings that are derived from mayonnaise.

Mayonnaise and its Derivations

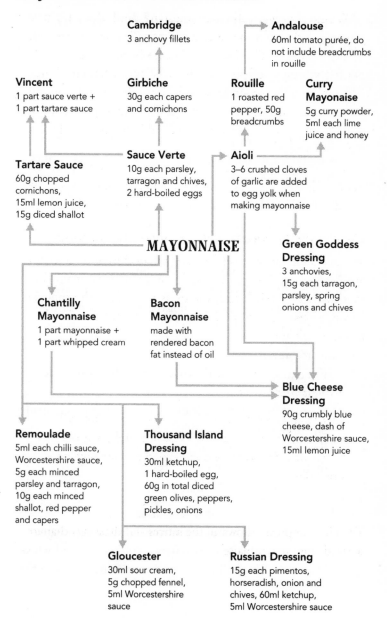

Cambridge
3 anchovy fillets

Andalouse
60ml tomato purée, do not include breadcrumbs in rouille

Vincent
1 part sauce verte + 1 part tartare sauce

Girbiche
30g each capers and cornichons

Rouille
1 roasted red pepper, 50g breadcrumbs

Curry Mayonnaise
5g curry powder, 5ml each lime juice and honey

Tartare Sauce
60g chopped cornichons, 15ml lemon juice, 15g diced shallot

Sauce Verte
10g each parsley, tarragon and chives, 2 hard-boiled eggs

Aioli
3–6 crushed cloves of garlic are added to egg yolk when making mayonnaise

MAYONNAISE

Green Goddess Dressing
3 anchovies, 15g each tarragon, parsley, spring onions and chives

Chantilly Mayonnaise
1 part mayonnaise + 1 part whipped cream

Bacon Mayonnaise
made with rendered bacon fat instead of oil

Blue Cheese Dressing
90g crumbly blue cheese, dash of Worcestershire sauce, 15ml lemon juice

Remoulade
5ml each chilli sauce, Worcestershire sauce, 5g each minced parsley and tarragon, 10g each minced shallot, red pepper and capers

Thousand Island Dressing
30ml ketchup, 1 hard-boiled egg, 60g in total diced green olives, peppers, pickles, onions

Gloucester
30ml sour cream, 5g chopped fennel, 5ml Worcestershire sauce

Russian Dressing
15g each pimentos, horseradish, onion and chives, 60ml ketchup, 5ml Worcestershire sauce

All recipes start with 240ml base

How to combat antisocial behaviour in sauces

- If it's lumpy sieve it, or use a blender to smooth it, then simmer for 5 minutes.

- If it's too thin simmer to reduce it, or, if you are pressed for time, mix ½ tablespoon flour into a paste with ½ tablespoon butter then add it to the sauce while off the heat and whisk till fully combined.

- If it's too thick, beat in a few tablespoons of liquid (hot water, vegetable cooking liquid, stock, milk, or cream) one at a time till it's thinned out.

- If your egg-based sauce curdles, this is either from too much acidity or because when the eggs were introduced to the sauce, the liquid was so hot the eggs cooked instead of incorporating.

- How to prevent curdling:
  - If making a sauce with wine, eggs and cream – add the wine *first*.
  - Beat the eggs with a bit of cold water before gradually blending in the hot liquids.
  - Beat the eggs with a small amount of the heated sauce, then add this mixture to the rest of the sauce.
  - Use a dairy product with a higher fat content.

- How to stop curdling once it's started:
  - Sometimes just removing it from the heat is enough.
  - If not, add a bit of cold water or cold cream and whisk like mad – this will lower the temperature and stop the curdling.

* Fill your sink with cold water, and if your sauce looks as though it is about to curdle, take the pan off the stove and hold it in the cold water while you stir very fast. This should cool it down and stop the curdling.

> If the sauce has separation anxiety it could be caused by excess acidity. Try reducing the amount you are using. Cream-based sauces can be stabilised with extra cream if they look as though they're going to separate.

Some final tips on storage

* Stocks, tomato, velouté, béchamel and brown sauces keep in the fridge for a week or more and they can all be frozen.

* Small containers, freezer storage bags and ice trays work well for freezing smaller portions.

* Hollandaise can be refrigerated or frozen. If frozen, thaw in the fridge. To reconstitute, gradually heat 2 tablespoons of it, then beat in the rest a spoonful at a time. It can also be used to enrich a béchamel or a velouté. Beat it into a heated sauce a spoonful at a time, just before serving.

* Label them. Lots of sauces look the same frozen.

Chapter three

.

Vegetables and Fruit

The vegetables we serve with our meals are often just an afterthought. This can result in a terribly prepared, lousy-tasting vegetable. Your vegetables would like you to join the revolution and treat them with as much peace, love and understanding as any other food you prepare. Eat your greens, reds, oranges, yellows or purples and get to know how best to cook them. You can make stupefying feats of flavour and presentation with them.

Our vegetable manifesto

1. Vegetables need to – nay, will – step out of their former place as a side dish and take their rightful place as an occasional main course.

2. Vegetables refuse the abuse of past centuries of being boiled, parboiled or left to rot in the fridge.

3. No person shall ever again underestimate the power of properly prepared vegetables!

4. Vegetables will have it be known that they would love to be grown in your garden (if you have the space).

5. Vegetables hate travel and get less tasty when they have to.

The great debate: fruit or vegetable?

And all the confusion that can cause. Fruit is defined as the edible part of the plant that contains seeds, and vegetables are the stems, tubers or leaves of a plant that can be eaten. So in botanical terms tomatoes, cucumbers, squash, avocados and many other plants we commonly think of as vegetables are actually fruits.

Top ten veg (in alphabetical order)

Experimenting with cooking vegetables was a huge part of the cooking challenge for both of us. If there was ever an area that needed more love and attention, this was it. There was even quite a bit of vegan cooking, which was something that neither of us had attempted before. We love veg, and here are some great ones.

Artichokes

2000 years ago, some hungry Italians decided to eat a thistle, liked it, and have cultivated it ever since. Eat them as soon after buying them as possible because they become stringy as they age. If you are growing them in your garden, remember that once they flower they become inedible but make for a great centrepiece. To prepare them for cooking you can go minimal or extreme.

- **Minimal:** remove all the outer leaves at the base, and then, using scissors, snip the top off of each leaf. Remove as much of the fibrous centre as you can.

- **Extreme:** remove all the outer leaves, dig out all the fibrous matter on the heart and trim down until just the heart remains.

Best ways to cook
- **Poach:** simmer in water or one part water one part olive oil for 20 minutes. Adding lemon juice to the water helps reduce oxidisation and keeps the artichoke a bright green.

- **Grill or bake:** poach as above for 10 minutes, then chop the artichoke in half and grill it. Or stuff with grains, breadcrumbs, meat or a combination and bake for 20 minutes at 180°C/gas mark 4.

Lovely flavour combinations
Anchovies, bacon, breadcrumbs, butter, cream, fennel, garlic, lemon, mayonnaise, Parmesan, pine nuts, olive oil, walnuts, white wine.

Aubergines

Not always aubergine in colour, they are available as large globes, elongated and thin, Chinese or Asian and in the mini-egg-shaped and baby varieties. Larger aubergines should be chopped and soaked in cold salt water for 20 minutes, then dried. This removes any bitter flavour and mild allergens. With smaller ones, you can skip this.

Best ways to cook

Confit, gratin, sautée, deep fried covered in garlic sauce. To make the dip called baba ganoush: roast whole over an open flame until it is deflated and the skin is black, remove the soft interior and mix with tahini, garlic, olive oil, lemon juice and salt.

Lovely flavour combinations

Basil, beef, capers, garlic, ginger, goat's cheese, lamb, marjoram, mozzarella, onions, oregano, Parmesan, parsley, pine nuts, pork, ricotta, sausage, shallots, sour cream, soy sauce, tahini, thyme, tofu, tomatoes, tomato sauces.

Corn

Every bit of the corn cob can be used to make oils, sweeteners, bourbon whisky, grains and flour. It is the largest crop in all of the Americas.

Best ways to cook

Stop boiling it! It makes it less delicious than it otherwise is. Corn is great roasted on or off the cob, grilled or chopped off the cob and sautéed over a medium to low heat with olive oil, butter and salt until it caramelises. Purée it, mix it with cream and sugar and make it into ice cream or ice pops. Avoid tinned corn. It is a pale soggy shadow of fresh corn. Frozen corn is good even if freezer burnt (that's frostbite, for food). It makes a good icepack for a burn or injury.

Lovely flavour combinations

Bacon, basil, butter, Cheddar, crab, cream, edamame, ground black pepper, jalapeno peppers, lobster, mushrooms, onions, poultry (roasted), red peppers (roasted), sugar, tarragon, tomatoes.

Corn smut

Huilacoche or corn smut is a fungal disease that grows on corn and is very contagious. Farmers who want to avoid it spreading pick the offending corn cobs and bury them away from the field. The same fungus growths are a delicacy in Mexico, tasting like mushrooms and going well in tacos and quesadillas.

Mushrooms and truffles

Store mushrooms in the fridge and not in plastic or they will get slimy fast. To clean wild mushrooms, put them in a bowl, cover with cold water, shake vigorously, and then double-check they are clean. You can just brush the dirt off cultivated mushrooms. Shiitake mushrooms have a very hard stalk, so always remove it. All mushroom trimmings are excellent for stocks. Dried mushrooms can be rehydrated whenever you want to add mushroom flavour to a stir fry or sauce. Save the water you used to rehydrate the mushrooms. Sieve it through a paper towel to remove any grit, and reduce it by half, then it too can be saved for a sauce, added to stock or used to poach truffles in. Black truffles can be poached in mushroom stock and frozen until you need them. White truffles need to be stored in a damp towel inside an airtight container. Don't store them in rice – as many places do – because it dries them out.

Best ways to cook

In sauces, sautéed, baked, stuffed or eat them raw ... is there anyway we don't like them? Fry over high heat with a bit of oil and salt. As they cook, they first absorb the oil, then they release liquid. If the pan is too crowded you will wind up with tons of liquid, if there is more room and the heat is high, the liquid will evaporate as it comes out and the mushrooms will be brown and meaty and awesome. If you add a small splash of lemon juice, it will enhance the flavour without actually making the mushrooms taste lemony. If you have way too many, freeze them and use in stock. You could also slice them up and marinade in vinaigrette (see page 85 for a recipe) overnight.

Lovely flavour combinations

Anchovies, basil, bread, butter, capers, cheese, chives, cream, dill, eggs, garlic, meat, mustard, nutmeg, olive oil, olives, onions, oregano, pasta, poultry, shallots, sour cream, soy sauce, thyme, tofu, tomatoes, wine.

Portobello mushrooms were popularised in the 1980s as
a way to sell crimini mushrooms which most growers at
the time considered overly mature.

Onions, shallots and garlic

Are all part of the allium family. Shallots are not half onion,
half garlic – a common misconception – they are their own
things. Onions and leeks contain allicin, a natural antibiotic
for fighting infection, sulphur which is good for the liver and
a natural blood thinner that helps lower blood pressure. They
can be stored in or out of the fridge. Save all onion, shallot
and garlic trimmings, including skins, for stock. If you spray
garlic juice on your skin while pressing or smashing garlic and
you don't wipe it off, it will burn.

Ways to avoid onion tears that may or may not be true:

1. Hold some water in your mouth while cutting them,
   or just keep you mouth shut.

2. Chop them near an open flame or candle.

3. If your eyes are irritated stick your head in the
   freezer.

4. A very sharp knife may reduce the amount of
   crying.

Best ways to cook

Roasted very slowly, caramelised, deep fried, gratin, confit.

Lovely flavour combinations

Apples, bacon, burgers, cloves, mushrooms, hot peppers, meat, paprika, pineapple, poultry, pulses, tamarind – they go with almost everything, actually.

Peppers

All peppers start out green – green bell peppers are under-ripe red or yellow bell peppers.

Best ways to cook

Grilled, roasted, sautéed, confit. If you want to roast peppers, you can do it either under the grill, in the oven or on the hob. Heat them until they turn black, then leave them in a bowl covered with clingfilm till they cool down enough to touch. Next, peel off the skins, which should slide right off. Roasted peppers will keep for a long time if stored in a salt-water brine or submerged in oil.

Lovely flavour combinations

Anchovies, bulgur wheat, goat's cheese, coriander, corn, cucumbers, cumin, meat, rice, ricotta.

How to handle hot peppers

Chop them, then rinse the cutting board and knife immediately and wash the heck out of your hands. The seeds are the crazy hot part. Always be very aware of your hands: *never* touch your face or eyes. *Always* wash your hands straight afterwards. Some people wear rubber gloves.

Potatoes

There are about 600 varieties of potato. Most fall into one of two categories, waxy or floury:

- **Waxy:** new, Charlotte, pink fir apple, Jersey royal. They all hold their shape after cooking, so they're great for use in salads and for scalloped potatoes.

- **Floury:** King Edward, golden wonder, carat and Maris Piper have a sort of fluffy inside that makes them wonderful for chips, roasting and baking.

Unlike regular potatoes, sweet potatoes keep well in the fridge, freeze well and reheat like a dream.

Five good things to know about the potato

1. Store them in a cool dark place but not the fridge because it is cold enough to turn the potato's starch into sugar so they will spoil. Same deal with sunlight.

2. Once potatoes turn green they become mildly poisonous, so either toss them away or cut out the green parts.

3. New potatoes are harvested when still immature, leaving them with less starch and a very tender skin.

4. Always soak the saucepan you mashed the potatoes in right away, otherwise the residue turns to glue.

5. Fried or cooked potatoes freeze and reheat just fine. Raw potatoes in combination with other foods, as in stews, do not freeze well and turn to a grainy mush.

Best ways to cook

Roasted, sautéed, deep fried, mashed, baked, gratin, salads, grated and fried. Potatoes can be cooked in any way and with anything.

Food for the people

Potatoes were recognised by many governments as a food that would grow well and feed many, but the citizens didn't always take to them. One governor in Greece wanted to make potatoes more desirable to the common man, so he made a huge pile of them by the harbour and set up guards to watch them, but with the secret understanding that they would not watch them too well. By the next morning, all the potatoes were gone, and the whole area eventually had a reliable crop. Similar tactics were used in Paris and throughout Austria.

Lovely flavour combinations

Bacon, butter, cheese, chives, cumin, curry, duck fat, eggs, goose fat, gravy, hot peppers, ketchup, lemon, liver, mace, meat, mushrooms, nutmeg, onions, paprika, poultry, rosemary, sour cream, truffles, Worcestershire sauce.

Root vegetables

Carrots, turnips, parsnips, Jerusalem artichokes, swede and beetroot.

Most of these are winter vegetables and most of them are inexpensive, though Jerusalem artichokes can be a bit costly. They tend to go quite well in combination with each other, and though most of the time they are just thought of as the things that are under or round the roast, they are all wonderfully healthy, satisfying and delicious in their own right.

Best ways to cook

Roasted, sautéed (sometimes it helps to parboil them first), mashed, puréed, gratin, pickled or eaten raw. With parsnips, especially the really big ones, be sure to remove the core as it tends to be quite hard even when cooked. Be careful with beetroot because they stain with reckless abandon, so you might want to wear gloves when preparing them. Steam and purée a huge batch of carrots. They will sweeten and thicken while adding a vitamin-A boost and can be used in just about anything – soups, sauces, breads and pies.

True colours

Purple carrots used to be the norm; the orange ones were specially bred to match the colours of the Dutch royal family.

Eat enough beetroot and your pee will turn pink!

Lovely flavour combinations

Almonds, apples, bay, black pepper, blue cheese, butter, cinnamon, coriander, cream, cucumber, cumin, curry, dill, fennel, garlic, goat's cheese, honey, mushrooms, mustard seeds, onions, orange and orange zest, peanut butter, pork, port, poultry, sage, salmon, sesame seeds, sherry, smoked fish, sour ream, sugar, tamarind, thyme, walnut oil, walnuts.

Tomatoes

The Spanish introduced tomatoes into Europe from South America, but only grew them for decoration thinking they were members of the deadly nightshade family and therefore poisonous. As with artichokes, a brave Italian ate one and they have been making good stuff with them ever since. Tomatoes can be frozen whole, then used in place of tinned tomatoes in sauces, or they can be made into sauce, which freezes well too. Tinned tomatoes are great in recipes calling for chopped or diced tomatoes that you then cook. If a recipe calls for sun-blush tomatoes, pour boiling water over sun-dried tomatoes (cheaper and easier to find), leave for 20 to 30 minutes, then drain well.

Three ways to skin tomatoes

- Method 1: grate them. Cut them in half round their horizontal middles, then use a box grater. The skin will stay intact and protect your fingers as you go.

- Method 2: submerge them in rapidly boiling water until the skin pops, then shock them in cold water and peel the skin off.

- Method 3: put them in a bowl and cover with boiling water. Leave for 1 minute, then drain, shock with cold water and peel.

Best ways to cook

Confit, broiled, roasted, stewed, grilled or eat raw.

Lovely flavour combinations

Anchovies, bacon, balsamic vinegar, basil, black pepper, capers, crusty bread, couscous, currants, curry, eggs, garlic, mayonnaise, mint, pasta, olives, tarragon, tuna, raisins, walnuts.

Tomatoes of tomorrow?

There are strains of tomatoes that have been genetically modified and combined with fish genes to lengthen their shelf life. Yum.

Winter squash

Butternut and pumpkin are the two we see most frequently, but there are others with wildly different shapes, sizes and colours with funny names like Turk's turban, sweet dumpling and onion. Don't be afraid to try any type that is available. They can all be prepared using the same methods, some might just have slightly longer or shorter cooking times.

Get them open anyway you can. Squash are so hard you might have to take a hatchet to them. Fun! Remove all the stringy innards and seeds. Pumpkin seeds are delicious toasted and salted. Hulled seeds can be puréed, seasoned and added to a dip or pie filling.

Best ways to cook

Roast by cutting in half or into chunks and mix with butter, salt, pepper (and any other spices you fancy, or sugar if you like), then cover in foil and bake until very soft. Mash, purée, confit, gratin, make into soups. Roast, then mash and freeze them for use later on. Cold roasted squash is nice in salads, panini or mashed into patties and fried.

Lovely flavour combinations

Almonds, bacon, brown sugar, cheese, chestnuts, cinnamon, curry, dried apricots, ginger, ham, hazelnuts, honey, nutmeg, olives, oranges, pecans, pineapple, port, rosemary, sage, smoked hot peppers, walnuts.

Know your source

Local

We are living in a true golden age of food, when almost anything we could possible want can either be bought in a shop or ordered and delivered to our door. This is great for expanding your culinary horizons, but this global food market is having an ecological impact. The further away the food you are eating is produced, the more fuel is needed to ship it and the more greenhouse gases are produced which equals global warming. Many vegetables have travelled half-way round the world in order to get onto our plates. Eating locally grown vegetables is better for the environment and it supports farmers in your area. It also means you know what you are buying is fresh and in season – which will always get you a more delicious vegetable.

Organic

Organic fruit and vegetables are grown without any pesticides or artificial fertilisers. But the organic label doesn't tell you whether they are genetically modified or heirloom (see below). Also, if when you think of organic, you picture a small vegetable patch being tending to by elderly monks this isn't likely. Lots of organic produce is grown on large-scale farms.

Heirloom

This means the vegetables are grown from seeds that are generally a very old variety and so are non-hybrid and always genetically unmodified. These are seldom grown on large-scale farms.

If it all seems too much to take on board, try starting small. Buy apples that have a British label, pick up some organic vegetables when they look good, ease your way into it.

> If you are buying organic vegetables, wash them instead of peeling them – you'll get loads more nutrients. If you are not buying organic, then peel don't wash, or you will be eating pesticide.

You mean you don't just boil them?

Lara's three-step roasting method

1. Make a marinade for your vegetables. It could be as simple as some fat and salt. If you want a more elaborate marinade, it should consist of a fat, seasoning and another flavour like soy sauce, vinegar, syrup or honey. 120ml of marinade per kilo of vegetables is plenty.

2. Coat the vegetables in the marinade and let them infuse for a while or . . .

3. Go ahead and put them straight in the oven. Here are the times and temperatures:
   - For root vegetables or Brussels sprouts: 200–250°C/gas mark 6–7 for 30 minutes to an hour. Turn them midway through cooking.
   - For most other vegetables like peppers, summer squash, mushrooms, tomatoes: 225°C/gas mark 7 for 10 to 30 minutes. Turn midway through cooking.
   - It's better to cook asparagus, green beans and corn under

the grill. Coat them with marinade and grill until they start to brown. Turn halfway through cooking. They don't take long, between 7 to 20 minutes. Check them every 2 minutes or so.

Roasted vegetables are good covered in a sauce, on sandwiches, as a side dish, made into a sauce, eaten hot, cold or in-between. You can store leftover roast vegetables in a salt-water brine or oil, or just in a big tub in your fridge.

Caroline's confit

Confit is very similar to roasting, and is one of the oldest ways of food preservation involving heat. It can also be incredibly delicious. Vegetables are immersed in a liquid – vegetable or animal fat, wine, stock, syrup, juice that can be infused with herbs, salt, sometimes sugar – then cooked until all the liquid has been absorbed. You can confit meat, fruit and vegetables. If you are planning a large meal for many people and find you have to do it over many days vegetable confit will happily sit in the fridge for some time before it is served and, as a bonus, this improves the flavour. It also sounds fancy. You can cook confit in the oven, on the hob, or a combination of both. Whatever you find works best for you.

How to make your own confit

- Choose a vegetable and a liquid you think make a good combination (refer to the flavour combinations for each vegetable). Pick some seasonings, herbs, spices, maybe another vegetable that goes with your primary one. For example: tomatoes + olive oil and wine + thyme, marjoram, garlic, diced roasted red peppers = delicious.

- Prepare the vegetable: slice, chop, maybe peel. Consider how you might like to arrange it in a baking or casserole dish – perhaps a millefeuille or soldier-style arrangement or just toss it in a casserole or flat dish.

- Prepare enough of the liquid and mix with the seasoning. It is up to you how much liquid you want absorbed into the vegetable you are preparing. The more liquid you add, the longer it will take to absorb.

- Cook it. Start at 150°C/gas mark 2. If the vegetables seem to be getting overdone before the liquid is absorbed, turn it down. If is seems the opposite, turn it up.

- Cook until the liquid is almost completely absorbed. Best let it sit overnight for the flavours to marry. Serve hot or cold.

Gratins and casseroles

Generally what comes to mind is the popular gratin of vegetables, but gratins also include lasagne, moussaka or scalloped potatoes, for example. In principle they are very similar to confit, but often include a béchamel or maybe a tomato sauce and/or some cheese. The gratin may be sprinkled or mixed with herbs, breadcrumbs, gremolata (see page 128 for recipe) or nuts. It can include pasta, grains, rice, meat, hard-boiled egg or a combination of any of these. Basically you are taking one or several vegetables and turning them into a delicious casserole. For most gratins the flavour improves over time and they are best served at room temperature. They are a good choice for transporting because they travel well. Make the dish at home and, if you can count on oven space at your destination, reheat once you get there.

How to make a gratin

- Prepare the vegetables: chop, slice, quarter – whichever you please. Next, either roast, sauté, blanch or mash them. You choose which. This gets the cooking process started, and reduces any bitter taste or excess starch. If you are boiling, drain the heck out of it, then pat it dry.

- Add whatever spices or seasonings go with the vegetables. You can choose your own, or refer to our lovely flavour combinations.

- In an ovenproof casserole or baking dish with high sides, combine the vegetables and sauce with anything else you are making your gratin with. If you arrange the vegetables in layers add sauce between them.

- Use about 250ml of sauce to every 500g vegetables for 4 people. You can use more or less.

- Top with something crispy like breadcrumbs or nuts, or with something melty like cheese or with both.

- Cook at 180°C/gas mark 4. Cooking time depends on the size and depth of your gratin. For deeper, heavier ones, cover for most of the baking time, then cook uncovered for the last 15 minutes to let the top brown properly. For lighter ones, made out of mashed vegetables, bake for 20 to 30 minutes uncovered until the top browns.

When you have too many vegetables to cook

Pickling

This is a nice way of preserving a vegetable when you have too much of it.

Quick Pickle

Good for carrots, beetroot, radishes.

> 60g sugar
> 60ml distilled white vinegar
> ¼ teaspoon salt
> 450g vegetables, cut in julienne or batons or grated

Whisk the first three ingredients together in a large bowl until dissolved. Add the vegetables and mix well. Stand at room temperature for 2 hours. Put into a clean, sterilised jar (you can do this by boiling the jar and top) with an airtight lid. Cover and chill. Good on sandwiches, in salads and as a tiny side dish. These can be kept for 2–3 weeks, chilled and covered.

Long Haul Pickle

Good for cauliflower, okra, French beans, asparagus, carrots or even turnips. As for the spices, use as much or as little as you would like of each. Pickles are a very individual thing. If you love garlic, go crazy with the garlic.

> clove of garlic, peeled
> handful or two of pearl onions, peeled
> head of cauliflower, leaves and core removed and
>   broken into florettes
> dried hot chilli pepper
> bay leaf
> coriander seeds
> dill
> tarragon
> sugar, if you swing that way
> 450ml red wine vinegar
> couple pinches of salt

Put the vegetables and spices into a sterilised jar. In a saucepan boil the vinegar and salt for 1 minute then pour enough into the jar to cover the vegetables. Seal. Hide in a cool dark place and forget about it for a few of months. Suddenly remember when craving pickles.

Large pan blanching

Not to be mistaken with boiling vegetables into oblivion. It's good for vegetables like broccoli, spinach, courgettes, green beans and Brussels sprouts to make them ready for freezing. Drop the vegetables into the boiling water, then almost immediately take them out again. When vegetables are cooked for more than a couple of minutes, they oxidise and lose their bright colour. This method can enhance the colour of some vegetables like green beans and broccoli, for instance. Sometimes blanching is done to help peel them – as with tomatoes; sometimes it's done before cooking them another way so they keep their beautiful colour; and it's a way of sterilising them so they can be tinned or frozen.

- Bring a huge pot of water to a rolling boil.

- Toss in the vegetables for 1 minute max.

- Drain the vegetables through a colander and immediately submerge them in a bowl of ice-cold water to stop them cooking further, otherwise called 'shocking' a vegetable.

Top ten tips about fruit

1. Apples and bananas both give off ethylene, a natural compound that speeds up the ripening process of other fruits and vegetables. On the up side this means that if you put a piece of under-ripe fruit in a paper bag with a banana, it will ripen more quickly. Unfortunately it also means that it might over-ripen or cause deterioration, not only in other fruits, but in green vegetables as well. Be sure to store apples in a separate refrigerator compartment from the green vegetables, or in a sealed plastic bag.

2. If you have lemons or limes that have been hanging around for a while, and it doesn't look like you are going to need them, you can freeze their juice for later. Squeeze them and remove any pips, then pour the juice into ice-cube trays. When it's frozen you can dump the ice cubes

into freezer storage bags and they will keep for months. Just don't forget to label them.

3. Medjool dates (the really nice-looking ones) may be a little more expensive, but if you keep them refrigerated in an airtight container, they will last up to a year.

4. Good-quality grapes can be frozen in bunches and eaten frozen as little ices for dessert. You can also lay them out on a tray and freeze. If you transfer them to an airtight container and store in the freezer, they will keep for up to 3 months. Just don't try to thaw them out, they won't have a very nice texture.

5. For a quick but fancy-looking dessert or dessert garnish, wet the cut sides of the fruit by dipping them into either rum, brandy or orange juice, then press them into brown sugar, and grill them, cut side up, for 8 to 10 minutes. They will look beautiful and taste good too.

6. Some fruits discolour when exposed to air. To prevent this, just toss them with a bit of lemon juice.

7. You can peel peaches just like you would tomatoes. Drop them into boiling water for 15 seconds to a minute, depending on how ripe they are. The skins will peel right off. You can do the same with grapes too, but only leave them in the water for about 10 seconds. Peeled grapes, as well as being safer for babies, also make great 'eyeballs' for Halloween parties.

8. To make pretty little pineapple rings like you see in pictures: peel the pineapple by first cutting off the top, then cutting across the bottom so it has a flat surface to stand on. Run a knife down till you've removed all the skin and

little 'eyes' that are sometimes left behind. Cut it into slices across the middle. Use a small biscuit cutter to cut out the centre.

9. Making a mango hedgehog is a really easy way to prepare an otherwise intimidating fruit. Hold the mango standing upright, and cut down, cutting off a chunk as close to half of the mango as you can, avoiding the huge pit inside. Then cut through the mango flesh, but not the skin, in horizontal then vertical lines and turn it inside out. Pull the square chunks off the skin (or cut them off if it's not quite ripe enough).

10. To open a coconut: find one that you can hear a lot of milk sloshing around in. Poke out the eyes, drain it and put it in the oven at 180ºC/gas mark 4 for 30 minutes. The heat will cause it to split and release the meat from the shell.

Ratatouille

~

The vegetable manifesto talked a big game, so here is a lovely dish that is completely vegetable, and delicious.

3 tablespoons olive oil
1 clove garlic, minced
2 shallots, diced
325g tinned diced tomatoes
   (or fresh tomatoes, peeled
   and chopped)
3 tablespoons carrots, grated
½ teaspoon marjoram
1 bay leaf
2 red peppers, roasted and
   diced or rinsed and dried if
   from a jar

½ teaspoon salt
3 beef tomatoes
1 courgette
1 Chinese aubergine
1 yellow squash
2 tablespoons olive oil
1 teaspoon balsamic vinegar
½ teaspoon of thyme
½ teaspoon oregano
salt and pepper

- First you make a base sauce. In a frying pan put the olive oil, garlic and shallots over a low to medium heat. Cook until soft, 7 to 9 minutes. Add the tomatoes, carrots, marjoram, bay leaf. Simmer for 10 minutes. Lower the heat and add the peppers. Cook just long enough to combine the flavours. Remove from the heat and discard the bay leaf. In a round or oval casserole dish (20–24 cm), evenly spread the sauce. Meanwhile, using a mandolin or very sharp knife, slice the beef tomatoes, courgette, aubergine and squash as thinly as possible – less than a centimetre thick. Layer the vegetables in the dish in a spiral formation, slightly overlapping towards the centre. Keep going until either you have used all the vegetables, or the pan is filled.

Sprinkle with the oil, vinegar, thyme, oregano, salt and pepper.

- Cover with either the lid or a couple of layers of foil and bake at 150°C/gas mark 2 for 1½ hours. Remove the lid and return to oven for another 10 minutes. This dish can be made a day ahead. Serve from the dish hot or cold.

Chapter four

·

Pulses

Red beans and ricely yours.

LOUIS ARMSTRONG, American musician (1901–1971)

(he loved red beans and rice so much he signed his personal
letters thus)

Beans have been considered so useless that a hill of them
is worth nothing and counting them is equivalent to a
waste of time. This is not the case. Beans are magic.

There are about 12,000 plant species that fall under the
heading legume, but generally speaking, we eat pulses, or
peas, beans and lentils. Beans are wonderful and versatile and
oh, so good for you because they are rich in nutrients, low in
calories, high in fibre and we digest them slowly. This makes
them good for diabetics, dieters, people who need to lower
their cholesterol, and they may even help prevent cancer.
When combined with rice they form a complete, very healthy
protein.

> ### *Bean knowledge nugget number 1*
> In Japanese 'bean knowledge' is a colloquialism for
> a bunch of arbitrary, often useless knowledge.

Our favourite bean – the soya bean or edamame

This is the most versatile of beans, and is very good for you. Among all the fabulous things it contains, at the top of the list are the anti-carcinogens (which reduce your risk of cancer), and the omega 3 fatty acids (which reduce your risk of heart disease). If you are not eating enough oily fish or eggs then up your soya intake. You can find soya beans dried or frozen, shelled and still in the pod.

- Chinese black beans are fermented black soya beans.

- Japanese miso is made from fermented soya beans.

- Soy sauce is made with soya too, but some cheap brands of soy sauce don't actually have soya in them.

- Soya milk is made from dry soya beans that have been crushed, soaked and pressed. Sometimes sugar, vanilla and other flavours are added.

- Roast some in a low oven, about 130°C/gas mark 1 or 2, for just over an hour. Salt them if you prefer. They make great snacks!

Our favourite bean product – tofu or bean curd

Tofu is curdled soya bean mash. It is an incredibly versatile food. It can be marinated, stewed, deep fried, baked, prepared so it resembles custard or cheese. There are different textures of tofu: silken, soft, medium and firm. They are just as they are named. To store tofu you need to submerge it in water. If you are keeping it for a while, changing the water will help extend its shelf life. It has very little flavour on its own but its texture can be manipulated through a quick process of pressing, or freezing and thawing. It will also easily absorb any flavours it is marinated in.

How to make tofu taste delicious (no kidding)

Pressing tofu vastly improves its texture. Use firm or extra firm tofu:

- Drain, then wrap it in a cotton kitchen cloth.

- Place a baking sheet on top of it and something heavy, like cookbooks, on top of that. Leave for a minimum of an hour.

- Slice the tofu into 5mm to 1cm thick pieces. You can marinade them in just about anything and then bake, grill, fry or roast it. It will be very firm, somewhat chewy.

Bean knowledge nugget number 2

Castor and jequirity beans contain the most lethal poison occurring in nature. For centuries, those in the know have used them to kill people. These same beans are used to make necklaces and rosary beads.

Buying, keeping, preparing beans

Choosing the right beans

For fresh beans:

- Brightly coloured beans are usually fresher.

- Don't buy beans that are withered looking or floppy.

- Always cook beans as soon as they are shelled. Don't let them hang around.

- Similar-looking beans can be substituted for each other.

For tinned beans:

- Check to see what's keeping your beans company in the tin. Try to avoid beans tinned with sugar and excess salt or chemical preservatives, unless you are buying baked beans which need all that stuff to make them delicious.

- Beans are tinned with salt, so make sure you take that into consideration when seasoning your food.

- Tinned beans are already pretty soft, so you may need to add them to a recipe later than usual to avoid overcooking.

What to do with beans you just found at the back of your pantry

- Look for shiny beans of uniform size and colour.

- Most dried beans keep nicely for 6 months at least.

- Although many beans fade in colour when dried, if they are really washed-out-looking it may indicate they are very old.

- Tiny pinholes can mean an insect has already snacked on it, or made the bean its home.

- Discolouration round the eye, or hilum, of the bean is also a bad sign.

- If they are really old, they won't absorb liquid properly. This is especially true of chickpeas.

Know your lentils

Brown and green lentils hold their shape when cooked, so they are the ones you want for stews, side dishes or salads. Red lentils break down to a thick liquid when cooked. They are especially good for soups.

Rinsing

Dried beans need to be rinsed and it's also a great way to check for tiny stones. Tinned beans need to be rinsed to reduce their salt content and it also improves their flavour. You will also be rinsing away some of the stuff that gives you wind (ogliosaccharides) and makes them hard for some people to digest.

Soaking

You only have to soak dried beans, not fresh ones, and not dried split peas or lentils.

- Regular soak: put the beans in a bowl and cover with two or three times their volume of water. Soak for at least 8 hours. If they are going to be soaking for more then 12 hours, refrigerate them to prevent fermentation.

- Quick soak: put them in a saucepan and cover with two or three times their volume of water. Bring the water to a boil, simmer for two minutes, cover, remove from the heat and let them stand for a couple of hours.

Bean knowledge nugget number 3

In Spain beans used to be referred to as *carne de los pobres* – meat of the poor.

Some tips from Lara

- If any beans float to the top during the soaking process, just throw them away.

- The soaking water from kidney and soya beans should be discarded before cooking, then boil the beans for at least 10 minutes to get rid of any toxins.

- Dried beans will just about triple in volume during cooking, make sure there's room in the pot.

- If you forget you are soaking beans and discover them a couple of days later, it is likely they will have sprouted. This isn't a bad thing. The sprouting process increases their nutrients and makes them easier to digest. Rinse them and use them in salad if the sprouts are long. If they seem quite newly sprouted, just continue to use them as you were originally planning. But don't eat sprouted kidney beans or soya beans.

Something for all the butter bean haters

A good excuse to get out of eating your butter beans is to inform whoever is serving them to you that they have cyanide in them. Those commercially grown in Europe contain very low levels, but the ones grown in parts of South East Asia have up to 30 times the amount allowed in the West.

Portion calculator

Portion size has so much to do with what kind of dish it is, but a decent rule of thumb is 65–80g dried beans per person.

Various methods of bean cookery

Each bean has a flavour and texture of its very own but they are a nice vehicle for other flavours. Beans like to be cooked in some sort of liquid medium. Water works, but so does stock, wine, beer, coconut milk, colas, vegetable purées, juices … you can use any of these when baking or boiling beans.

Bean knowledge nugget number 4

The name haricot, when you are talking about beans, comes from the Aztec word for kidney bean ayecotl. When you are talking about a haricot of beef (or other meat), the word, although the same, is derived from the French *harigoter,* meaning to mince, or cut up finely.

Caroline's favourite bean flavour combinations

Savoury: bacon, carrots, celery, chillies, garlic, ham bones, herbs, hot sauce, mustard, onion, oregano, ajwain seeds – which are reputed to reduce wind.

Sweet: apples, brown sugar, cinnamon, maple syrup, molasses, tomato paste.

· A TIP FROM CAROLINE ·

Adding salt to beans is a great way to bring out their flavour, but don't add it till at least halfway through the cooking time. It's even better to wait to the end. The same advice goes for any acidic flavouring you may be thinking of adding. If you add either too early it will toughen the skins.

Three ways to reduce wind

1. Try flavouring your dish with aniseed, bay leaves, cloves, cumin, epazote or stinkweed, savory or thyme. All these ingredients are rumoured to reduce the amount of wind you experience after eating beans.

2. Do not cook beans in their soaking water; drain them and cook them in fresh water instead. This reduces the harder-to-digest carbohydrates in the skins. Unfortunately, it also reduces the level of water-soluble B vitamins, but you can switch back to using the soaking water once your body is used to having beans regularly. If you are making kidney or soya beans, always discard the soaking water.

3. Eat more beans. Evidence shows that the more often you eat them, the more easily your body will digest them.

Boiling or stewing

Tinned beans are already cooked, so stewing them is a good way to marry them with other flavours, but there is no specific amount of time you have to cook them for them to be finished. Dried beans need to be boiled first. To reduce the foam that forms on the surface of the water when cooking beans, add a tablespoon of oil to the pot (or just skim the foam off the surface).

The skins of beans and lentils can easily break, leaving them less appealing to look at and less appealingly textured as well. Here are three ways to avoid trouble:

1. Shock the beans with cold water as they cook. This means a few times during cooking, throw a cup of cold water into the pot. This keeps the beans tender, but the skins intact.

2. Most of the time you will be told to boil the beans rapidly for the first 10 minutes or so, but after that it is really important to turn the heat down. The remainder of the cooking time they should be at a gentle simmer to avoid breakage.

3. Some sources will tell you to put a little bicarbonate of soda in the cooking water. It helps to soften the skins and make them slightly more digestible. On the other hand, it also destroys a portion of the vitamin content, specifically thiamine (vitamin B_1).

Caroline's three-step recipe for baked beans

Try this with any pulse, but some of my favourites are haricot, lentils, black beans, kidney, cannellini or pinto. Preheat oven to 180°C/gas mark 4.

1. Soak and then boil dried beans for 10 minutes. Tinned beans can be used straight away.

2. Put them into a casserole or ovenproof dish with whatever other ingredients you want to flavour them with (see flavour combinations above). Then add some liquid. This could be stock, chopped tomato, wine, beer, honey, maple syrup, any leftover sauce you have in your freezer or any combination of those. If you desire a more casserole end product, add about ¼ as much liquid as there are beans. If you prefer a stew consistency, make your beans swim in it.

3. You could layer the beans with rashers of bacon, peanuts, or cheese, and then top them with anything that will toast nicely, such as garlicky breadcrumbs or nuts (add a bit of fat, like olive oil or duck fat to the breadcrumbs so they bake instead of burn). If you want to add green herbs, do this towards the end unless they are well mixed with another topping ingredient. Put in the oven. Bake until the top is looking golden and the whole dish is bubbling and the liquid looks as though it has been either partly absorbed by the beans or has thickened.

Bean knowledge nugget number 5

Native Americans used to grow beans and corn next to each other because they had a symbiotic relationship. The beans would climb the corn as they would a trellis and in return released nitrogen which the corn needs to grow.

Storage

Cooked beans keep for about a week in the fridge, and can be frozen. That's why it's a good idea to make a bigger batch than you actually need. They are great for throwing in with all kinds of other things.

Freezing pre-soaked beans is an incredibly handy trick if you want to have some beans readily available. Soak the beans as you normally would. When the time is up, drain them, dry them off, and place them all in one layer on a sheet or container that will fit in your freezer. Leave to freeze so they are completely hard, then you can dump them into a freezer bag until you need them. When it comes time to use them, just drop the frozen beans directly into water that is already boiling. It should only take about 30 to 45 minutes for them to cook. Remember, they will have already done most of their bulking up during the initial soaking, so they shouldn't expand too much during cooking.

> ### *Bean knowledge nugget number 6*
>
> Robert Burton, author of *The Anatomy of Melancholy*, was no fan of the bean. He wrote, 'All pulse are naught, beans, peas, vetches, etc. they fill the brain with gross fumes, breed black thick blood and cause troublesome dreams.' He goes on to list 64 different ways to cure wind.

Cook your way through history: ancient Rome

This is a recipe from the ancient Roman and quite possibly oldest known cookbook *De Re Coquinaria* by Apicius.

Fabaciae Virides et Baianae (Green and Baian Bean)

    500g soya beans with pod, or green beans
    50ml liquamen (a salty fish sauce), or ½ teaspoon salt
      with 50ml wine
    1–2 tablespoons oil
    1 tablespoon minced coriander leaves
    1 teaspoon cumin seeds
    ½ minced branch of leek

Cook the beans with liquamen, oil, leek and spices. Serve.

Chapter five

·

Salads and Sandwiches

To make a good salad is to be a brilliant diplomatist – the problem is entirely the same in both cases. To know exactly how much oil one must put with one's vinegar.

OSCAR WILDE

Salad

Everybody has a slightly different notion of what makes a salad. A quote from US Supreme Court Justice Potter Stewart, writing about obscenity in the movies, comes to mind: 'I shall not today attempt further to define the kinds of material . . . But I know it when I see it.'

Salad is a little like that – hard to define, but you know it when you see it. Where salad used to mean just a wedge of lettuce with some salad cream, it can now be as elaborate and elegant as any other part of the meal, or a meal in and of itself. But, as in any other area of cooking, once you learn a few basics you can bend them and reinvent at will – like a pro.

Always use the freshest ingredients for a salad. Save the less fresh for cooking. That's not to say that disposing of your leftovers in a salad isn't a good idea. Blanched, roasted and confit vegetables are all good salad fodder.

Greens – way beyond iceberg

- baby spinach: tender and mildly flavoured; very vitamin and mineral rich

- chicory/curly endive/frisée: coarse and green, looks almost frizzy; can be very bitter

- cos or romaine lettuce: long, very crunchy leaves; stands up to thicker dressings; keeps a long time in the fridge

- dandelion: nice slightly wilted

- endive (Belgian or red): very crunchy, bitter; good chopped; nice base for hors d'oeuvres.

- escarole: slightly bitter, sturdy leaves, good cooked too

- iceberg: very crunchy; lasts a long time in the fridge; very mild flavour

- little gem: prematurely harvested cos

- lollo rosso: beautiful red curly leaves; very mild flavour

- mâche/lamb's lettuce/corn salad: sprigs with clusters of leaves, delicate, lovely, bittersweet

- mesclun: a mixture of greens that have been harvested early

- mustard leaf: pungent and peppery; good cooked and wilted

- radicchio/treviso: red leaves that are crispy, bitter; lasts well in the fridge; very nice shredded

- rocket: peppery, spicy, soft leaves; baby rocket is downright pungent; good when mixed with other greens; good with sharp or sweet dressings, can stand up to mustard/horse-radish

- butterhead lettuce: soft, tender; good for most dressings and sandwiches

- watercress: peppery, good in combination with other leaves, very strong; good for soups and sauces too

Salad herbs

Basil, chives, coriander, green onions, mint, parsley, sorrel.

Salad leaf tips

- Only clean your greens shortly before using them. Cleaning them days in advance will lead them to spoil sooner.

- Particularly if you are getting leaves straight from the garden, you'll need to clean any insects out of them. Fill the sink with water, add a couple of tablespoons of salt and leave the leaves to soak for 20 minutes. Insects and some grit will sink to the bottom of the bowl. Drain, then re-fill the sink. Turn the leaves gently with your hands, lift them out into a colander. Drain well to avoid soggy watery dressing.

- If you don't have a salad spinner, put the leaves in a tea towel, go outside and swing the tea towel in huge circular motions over your head.

- Using a knife when preparing lettuce can cause the edges to brown, use your hands to tear it into pieces.

- Prepare your ingredients so they blend together well and easily sit on a fork (nothing too bulky).

Dressings

Everyone likes a different level of acidity and sweetness in their salad dressings, try making dressings in as many ways as possible to see what you like best. A good place to start is vinaigrette which is a vinegar and oil emulsion. Droplets of vinegar are suspended in an oil, which is the opposite way round to a mayonnaise:

Vinaigrette

1 clove of garlic, smashed (optional)
30ml vinegar of choice
90ml olive oil
1–5ml mustard of choice
salt and pepper

Variations: avocado – add ½ mashed, ripe avocado; bacon – use hot bacon grease for the oil part. Fry some fatty bacon chopped small until the fat runs. Remove the crispy bacon bits from the pan and add them to the salad, splash some vinegar into the pan (roughly half the amount of the fat), swirl and pour over the salad.

Some tips from Lara

- One way to test the sharpness of a salad dressing is to put a bit on the tip of your tongue and breath in sharply. It should make you cough. You want it to be slightly too strong, because the flavour will become more subtle when it is spread over a whole salad.

- Some dressings are best prepared in a blender. This can help the ingredients emulsify and will chop large chunks of garlic, onion, shallots, apples, celery, nuts, incorporating all the ingredients together.

- Other good add-ins for dressings are: honey, maple syrup, dried or fresh herbs, yoghurt, all citrus, fish sauce, chillies, ginger root, miso, soy sauce, sesame seeds, ketchup, relish, harrisa, pesto, spices (toasting the spices is a great idea).

- Things that will flavour and thicken a dressing are: tahini, any nut butter, grated carrot, apples, peanuts. Mustard has a good emulsifying effect that thickens a salad dressing.

Caroline's way of making a healthier dressing

A good way to reduce calories in a cream- or mayonnaise-based dressing is to replace ⅓ of the cream or mayo with an equal amount of celery or tofu, then combine them in a blender. Both tofu and celery have a very mild flavour and will thicken the same as mayonnaise or sour cream.

Lovely flavour combinations

Apple and fennel; tahini and lemon; miso and maple syrup; mint and coriander, basil or chillies; carrot and miso; avocado and shallot.

Olive oil is golden

- Homer (the ancient poet, not the cartoon character) called olive oil 'liquid gold'.

- Almond oil is gross. In some parts of the world, and we will not name names, almond oil is extracted from goats' faeces. Goats climb almond trees, eat the nuts then excrete them semi-digested. They are then treated and pressed to extract the oil. This is not a gourmet product available at any store near you.

How to make a good salad

A good salad is about balance of flavour and texture. You don't have to hit all the flavour notes, but try for a contrast, like salt/sweet or crunchy/soft.

- **chewy:** cold calamari, dried fruit, prawns, Brie, beans, lardons, rice, pasta, wheat berries, oil-cured olives, fresh mushrooms, day-old bread

- **crunchy:** croutons, nuts, sunflower seeds, almonds, celery, carrots in chunks, cucumber, cold green beans, raw cauli-flower, cashews, water chestnuts, raw corn, cabbage, snow peas, candied pecans, radish, celeriac, diced or sliced raw beetroots, kohlrabi

- **salt/savoury:** bacon, heart of palm, olives, capers, ancho-vies, fish sauce, cold and smoked fish, croutons, tinned tuna, cornichons, avocado, egg, turkey, cold rare roast beef, peanut butter, grilled mushrooms, day-old bread, beans,

Gouda and Jarlsberg cheese, cold salmon, sesame seeds, artichoke hearts

- **spicy:** fennel, garlic, green peppers, leeks, onions (of all colours), pickled peppers, pimento, radish, shallots

- **sweet:** oranges, peas, dried fruit, apples, mozzarella, roasted red pepper, pineapple, cashews, Swiss cheese, water chestnuts, roasted corn, shredded or pickled beetroots, candied pecans, pears, grapes, papaya, shredded coconut, mangoes

- **tangy:** grapefruit, blood oranges, feta, goat's cheese, Parmesan, Gorgonzola, Cheddar, blue cheese, pineapple, marinated artichoke hearts, sour cream, yoghurt, tomatoes, pomegranate, sun-blush tomatoes, raspberries, marinated mushrooms

Flavour vehicles

Things that are just nice to have there for a dressing to stick to: bamboo shoots, bean sprouts, couscous, mushrooms, noodles, potatoes, quinoa, tofu.

· A TIP FROM LARA ·

Some onions are very pungent. If you want to mellow them slice thinly and soak them in water for 10 minutes. If they are still too strong, change the water and soak for another 10 minutes.

Lovely flavour combinations

Bacon and pretty much anything; Emmenthal and peas; grapefruit and avocado; oranges and sweet onions or shaved fennel; orange, duck and sweet onions; peanuts or peanut butter and cabbage; potatoes and anchovies; prosciutto, mozzarella, melons or figs; salmon and lemon; smoked trout and avocado; spinach, bacon and apples; walnut, Gorgonzola and pear.

Flowers! Impress your guests! Astonish your family!

Use the whole flower from rocket, camomile, chives, honeysuckle, lavender, mustard, pansies, nasturtium, squash blossoms, violas and violets. Use just the petals of calendula (marigolds), daisies, geraniums and roses.

Garden in a jar

Sprouts are as easy as growing mould on bread. They are one of the most nutrient-dense foods on earth.

Use a large glass jar with holes poked in the lid or with cheesecloth secured over the mouth with a rubber band. Put the seeds or beans in the jar and add enough water to cover them. Soak overnight. Then dump the water, rinse the seeds once and drain. Rinse the seeds every 12 to 24 hours. Depending on what you are sprouting, they should take between 2 and 7 days to be ready to eat. Seeds that have been toasted won't sprout.

You can sprout any of the following:

- **seeds and nuts:** alfalfa, almonds, amaranth, annatto, anise, rocket, barley, basil, broccoli, canola, caragana, cauliflower, celery, chives, clover, coriander, cress, dill, fenugreek, fennel, flax, hemp, kale, mustard, psyllium, pumpkin seeds, quinoa, radish, sesame, spelt, sunflower

- **beans and grains:** azuki, broad beans, black-eyed peas, buckwheat, chickpeas, green peas, lentils, mung beans, navy beans, oats, pearl millet, pigeon peas, pinto beans, wheat berries

Note: Never ever eat sprouted kidney or soya beans. They are very toxic

Make your own croutons

Plain croutons are just some bread cut into cubes, tossed with a bit of oil and baked at 170°C/gas mark 3 for 10 to 15 minutes. Herbed ones are made by putting herbs and spices, say minced garlic, rosemary and thyme in a pan with some oil, heating until fragrant then adding the cubed bread and coating well, followed by the trip into the oven.

Make your own lardons

Lardons are the pork equivalent to croutons. Cut pancetta or streaky bacon into 3cm cubes. Put the bacon into a saucepan with water, bring to a boil, count to 10 then drain. Heat a pan to high and fry the bacon until crispy. This method ensures you achieve a both chewy and crunchy consistency. The boiling adds the chewy, the frying crisps it up.

In 2007 the Guinness Book of Records recognised the province of Almeria in Spain as having made the worlds largest tossed salad, weighing in at 6,700 kilos. One wonders what size bowl they needed to make it.

A retro jelly salad

There was a period of time, not so long ago – I call it the Tupperware era – when jelly was considered a gourmet 'salad' base, always served from moulds resembling anything from a ring mould to a fish. Here is one of the more outlandish ones:

Chutney Chicken Salad in Avocado Lime Jelly

SERVES 4

For the jelly
1 packet lime jelly
100ml boiling water
100ml chicken stock or white
   wine
2 avocados
110g cream cheese
50g mayonnaise
juice of a lime
1 spring onion, sliced

FOR THE CHICKEN

500g chicken, cooked, cold,
   shredded
60g mayonnaise
60g mango chutney
juice of ½ a lime
salt
dash of curry powder

Put the jelly in a bowl and pour over the boiling water. Stir till the jelly melts, then add the stock or wine. Mash the avocados with the cream cheese, mayonnaise, lime juice and spring onion. Pour the jelly into the avocado and stir together. Pour into a 1 litre jelly ring mould. Chill for at least 4 hours.

In a bowl mix all the chicken ingredients and chill in the fridge.

Unmould the jelly over a nice arrangement of lettuce and fill the centre with chicken salad. Proudly serve!

Sandwiches

Legend has it that the sandwich was invented during a poker game by the Earl of Sandwich. He had a hot hand and was hungry but didn't want to leave the game to eat, and thought up – his head not being too filled with numbers and bluffing – the sandwich. But really, how likely is it that for the few thousand years before that no one thought that meat + something saucy surrounded by bread wasn't something to at least try. We won't insult you by telling you how to fill two pieces of bread. Instead, we'll give you this handy chart of classic sandwiches from around the world.

BÁNH MÌ

Bread – baguette made with 1 part rice flour 1 part wheat flour

Contents – pickled carrots and onions, cilantro, sliced cucumber, diakon, sliced meat, jalapeno

Condiments – mayonnaise, fish sauce

Variations – chicken, tofu, tripe or egg

Origin – Vietnam

Derivation – named after the bread

BLT

Bread – toasted white sliced bread

Contents – bacon, lettuce, tomato

Condiments – mayonnaise

Variations – with avocado is called a Californian BLT

Origin – United Kingdom

Derivation – named after its contents

CLUB

Bread – 3 slices of toasted bread

Contents – two sandwiches on top of one another sharing a 3rd slice of bread in the centre, sliced turkey, bacon, lettuce, tomato

Condiments – mayonnaise or mustard

Variations – ham, roast beef, tuna or chicken salad instead of sliced turkey

Origin – Saratoga, New York

Derivation – created at a private club, hence the name

CUBANO

Bread – grilled Cuban bread

Contents – roast pork, cured ham, pickle, Swiss cheese

Condiments – mustard

Variations – tomatoes, lettuce, salami

Origin – Cuba and Tampa, Florida

Derivation – named after Cuba

CROQUE-MONSIEUR

Bread – grilled white sliced bread

Contents – ham and Gruyère

Condiments – mustard, mornay, béchamel

Variations – Provençal is with tomato, auvergnat with blue cheese, tartiflette with sliced potatoes

Origin – France

Derivation – *croquer* is the French for 'to crunch'

CHEESESTEAK

Bread – long, white sandwich roll

Contents – grilled thinly sliced steak with thick orange sauce that is called 'cheese wiz'

Condiments – grilled onions, peppers, mushrooms and sometimes ketchup

Variations – chicken instead of steak, with barbeque sauce is called a Western

Origin – Philadelphia, Pennsylvania

Derivation – named after its contents

GYROS (also called kebab)

Bread – pitta, or other flat bread

Contents – vertical rotisserie meats, lettuce, tomato, onions

Condiments – tzatziki

Variations – addition of chips

Origin – Greece

Derivation – comes from the Greek word 'to turn'

SANDWICH DE MIGA

Bread – single or double sandwich with soft white crustless bread

Contents – thinly sliced meat, eggs, cheese, tomatoes, peppers, sliced olives

Condiments – mayonnaise

Variations – sometimes made with roasted red peppers, asparagus, other vegetables

Origin – Argentina

Derivation – named after the bread

SLOPPY JOE

Bread – hamburger bun

Contents – loose minced beef, tomato sauce, onions, spices

Condiments – N/A

Variations – can be made with minced turkey or textured vegetable protein

Origin – United States

Derivation – it is impossible to eat without making a mess

SMØRREBRØD

Bread – open sandwich made with rugbrød

Contents – cold cuts, bacon, herring, fish fillets, eggs, cucumber, tomato or pickled beetroot

Condiments – mayonnaise or toasted onion bits

Variations – huge number of variations

Origin – Denmark

Derivation – translates as 'butter and bread'

SUBMARINE*

Bread – long crusty roll similar to baguette

Contents – cured meats, cheese, lettuce, tomato, onion and various other veg, served hot or cold

Condiments – mayonnaise, mustard, salad dressings, salt, pepper

Variations – hundreds of local variations

Origin – United States

Derivation – named after the shape of the bread, has different names depending on where you are in the US

* Also called hero, hoagie, grinder, Italian beef

TORTAS

Bread – *bolillo* or *telera*, a soft but crusty roll

Contents – beans, crema, coriander, pickled jalapeno, avocado, hot spiced meat

Condiments – hot sauce

Variations – different types of grilled or roasted meat and sausages

Origin – Mexico

Derivation – Spanish for sandwich

Quesadilla [kay-sa-dee-yuh] – a Spanish sandwich

This is the Spanish word for a tortilla – it means a cheesy tiny thing. Tortillas are filled with cheese and anything else you can dream up to put in it. Traditionally they are made with corn but flour and whole wheat ones are great too. They are quick, easy, toasty, and a big favourite with the kids. Here's how to make one.

- On one half of the tortilla put cheese, beans, meat, salsa, vegetables – anything you feel like, really.

- Fold the tortilla in half. Heat a frying pan or grill to medium high and add some butter and extra virgin olive oil.

- Put the tortilla in the pan. Check the bottom every so often to see if it is browning, then flip it over once the first side is well toasted.

- Toast the other side until the cheese has melted, remove from heat, cut into wedges and serve.

Lovely Quesadilla flavour combinations

Beans, cheese, roasted corn and avocado (really good for breakfast if topped with a couple of fried or scrambled eggs); mole sauce (a popular Mexican sauce, made from bitter chocolate and chillies), chicken, Cheddar; sun-blushed tomatoes and goat's cheese; tomato sauce, mozzarella cheese and basil or pesto; leftover cooked broccoli and Cheddar; bacon and any kind of cheese; a sharp cheese with thinly sliced apple and cooked sausage.

Chapter six

·

Poultry

Poultry is for the cook what canvas is to the painter.

JEAN-ANTHELEME BRILLAT-SAVARIN, French politician,
lawyer and writer (1755–1826)

Chicken

Chicken facts

Chickens are considered to be the closest living
relatives to Tyrannosaurus Rex.

Chicken is one of the most popular proteins on the planet.
It is so ubiquitous that we compare all other flavours to it,
happily declaring 'it tastes like chicken' to any new food we
try that we don't find repugnant. Almost any flavour or food

will work with it, which means that you don't have to worry about what else you have in the fridge or cupboards, because whatever is there will go with it. When you are making a new recipe every day for a year, chicken can be your best friend. We cooked it in every different way imaginable, and with anything you can think of, and still never got tired of it.

> ### *Chicken facts*
>
> Chickens were one of the first domesticated animals. There is evidence of them being farmed in 6000BC – that's 8,000 years ago.

Know your source

BATTERY

Reared to – 41–43 days
Crowding – 17 chickens per square metre
Shelter – Caged, no access to outdoor runs
Diet – May contain antibiotics and growth hormones

EXTENSIVE INDOOR OR BARN REARED

Reared to – 56 days old
Crowding – 15 chickens per square metre
Shelter – In barns, no access to outdoor runs
Diet – May contain antibiotics and growth hormones

FREE RANGE

Reared to – 60–80 days
Crowding – 13 chickens per square metre

Shelter – Outdoor daytime access for half its life
Diet – Grain and feed pellets

TRADITIONAL FREE RANGE

Reared to – 81 days old
Crowding – 12 chickens per square metre
Shelter – Continuous daytime access from 6 weeks old
Diet – Grain and feed pellets

ORGANIC

Reared to – 80–90 days
Crowding – Varies
Shelter – Continuous daytime access on pesticide-free organic land
Diet – Organic grain and water

> Organic chickens are not plumped up with water, so they take a little longer to cook.

Four safety tips for chicken lovers

1. When shopping for chicken or any other type of fowl, avoid unusual amounts of liquid in the package and any trace of bad odour or stickiness.

2. If you are defrosting the bird in the fridge, allow a day for every 3 kilos of weight. A good indication that it is completely defrosted is that you should be able to wiggle it's legs and wings without resistance.

3. It's best to use a chicken within 48 hours of buying it. If it

is packed in an airtight package remove this before refrigerating.

4. Use different chopping boards for vegetables and meat. Most restaurants colour code their chopping blocks (maybe red for meat, blue for vegetables) to avoid confusion.

Chicken facts

There are more chickens on the earth than there are people.

Talking turkey

Turkeys, for the most part, can be prepared the same way that you would chicken. They are comparable in texture and fat content, have a slightly different flavour, but can be treated more or less the same, you just need a bigger pan. When it comes to raising practices, they are also, like chickens, often mistreated and raised in overcrowded environments. All the information regarding free range and organic chicken apply here as well.

Some turkey tips

• Buy turkeys with pearly white skin.

• Because of its larger size, and the longer cooking time required, whole turkeys have a tendency to dry out. Brining and barding (see below) are a couple of really great ways to tackle that problem.

Though turkey contains high levels of tryptophan (an essential amino acid), it is a myth that eating too much turkey will make you sleepy. The effects of the amino acid are only really notable when taken on an empty stomach, and yours would be full of turkey. Also, the levels are not actually any higher then those found in cheese.

Duck

Duck can be roasted, braised or grilled. They have a much higher fat content than chicken or turkey and have to be treated differently. While a chicken often benefits from cooking in its own juices, a duck does not and will become rubbery. In fact a duck releases so much fat that you have to pour it off a few times during cooking so it doesn't overfill the roasting pan.

Leftover cooked duck fat is called rendered duck fat. This is an extraordinary substance and can be used for all sorts of delightful purposes from roasting potatoes, or making pâté to replacing butter or olive oil in cooking.

Some tips from Caroline

- Before trussing, remove the fatty bit where the head used to be and the other fatty bit at the opposite end. Save. All duck fat is useful.

- Prick evenly or score the skin of duck. It helps the fat to drain more easily.

- Always cook duck on a rack.

- Salting heavily gives a crispy finish.

- Put metal utensils in the cavity of the duck. This increases the interior temperature, allowing more even cooking, reducing steaming and creating a crispier skin.

- Reduce the gamy flavour of duck by placing a potato or apple in the carcass while it roasts.

- Unlike chicken, do not cook duck breasts beyond medium rare or they will turn from tasty to tough.

Lovely flavour combinations

Almonds, apples, cherries, cinnamon, figs, five spice powder, garlic, ginger, grapefruit, green peppercorns, hoi sin sauce, honey, mangoes, orange, peaches, port, red wine, sage, soy sauce, mustard, prunes, plums, star anise, walnuts, white wine.

The golden goose

Not as commonly seen as duck, but becoming more and more popular for the holidays. At the moment geese are almost always free range because they are still only reared on a small scale. Cooking goose is very similar to duck; it also has an abundance of fat (and when rendered, is also exceptional for roasting potatoes), but a goose is much bigger than a duck, so before buying one, make sure it will actually fit in your oven. It should have a creamy-white appearance when you buy it, and will have a stronger, some say almost beefy flavour once cooked.

Turkey + duck + chicken = turducken

This fun amalgamation of three birds combined is based on a technique called ballotine and has, over recent years, risen in popularity as a dish for the holidays. This jokey title is actually no joke – a turducken is a boned turkey, stuffed with a boned duck, stuffed with a boned chicken. You can mix it up and use a goose in place of turkey. Often there is some sort of stuffing between the layers of poultry, specific to the type of poultry it is used under. You buy them prepared or, if you are a mad scientist type, make them yourself. Some more ambitious chefs (read total show-offs) don't stop at just three birds. In the *River Cottage Christmas Special 2007* Hugh Fearnley-Whittingstall made a ten-bird ballotine. If you want to try it yourself, he recommends using a turkey, then a goose, then any of the following birds: farmed duck, mallard, guinea fowl, chicken, pheasant, partridge, pigeon, woodcock.

Three ways your butcher can make your life easier

1. Boning: removing the bones, either from part or from a whole bird.

2. Jointing: cutting a whole bird into 6 or 8 portions. It's often cheaper then buying pre-packaged portions.

3. Spatchcocking: making a bird flat by opening it out like a book, and holding it in position with wooden or metal skewers. This reduces cooking time, making it perfect for grilling and barbecuing.

Chicken facts

Many early chicken farmers believed chickens to be sacred and of the sun. The Romans compared chickens to Mars, the god of war, because when they want to be, they are vicious.

Nifty things to do to a bird

A nice thing about poultry is that keeping it tender and making it delicious go hand and hand. Salt is a natural tenderiser because it breaks down the proteins in the meat. There are plenty of creative ways to get the salt and other tenderisers into your bird while improving flavour and adding texture.

Marinades

These tenderise the meat as well as adding flavour, but will not penetrate skin, so remove or slash the skin and flesh. Use just enough marinade to coat generously. Excess marinade can sometimes be reduced and turned into a sauce for the poultry. Marinades can be thick and stick to the bird while it is roasted or grilled, or can be thin and just add an oil and flavour for roasting, braising, pan frying or sautéing. If creating your own, consider making it a mix of sweet, sour and spicy or salty, sweet and smoky.

Great marinade ingredients

- For chicken and turkey: Armagnac, balsamic and red wine vinegar, barbecue sauce, beer, chives, cider, citrus juice, coconut milk, honey, maple syrup, olive oil, pineapple and mango juice, sesame oil, soy sauce, spring onions, sweet white wines.

- For duck: brandy, cranberry juice, Grand Marnier, hoi sin sauce, honey, mango and pineapple juice, olive oil, orange juice, port, sesame oil, soy sauce, tart cherry juice.

Dry rubs and pastes or meat lotion

Great for roasting, braising, sautéing, grilling. Dry rubs are a combination of various spices. Pastes are the same, but have some fat added to turn them from powder to paste. Massage them either onto the skin of the bird, or remove the skin and rub into the flesh. Pastes are particularly good with skinless chicken because the extra oils take the place of the skin. A classic dry rub is Jamaican jerk seasoning which is made from dried Scotch bonnet peppers, cloves, cinnamon and garlic.

- For chicken or turkey: anise, basil, cayenne pepper, chervil, Chinese five spice powder, cumin, dill, mint, mustard, oregano, parsley, paprika, Parmesan and asiago cheese, Peanuts, toasted crushed coriander seeds, wasabi.

- For duck: chillies, Chinese five spice powder, cinnamon, cloves, garlic, ginger, juniper berries, mustard, nutmeg, paprika, star anise.

Barding

For card-holding members of the Bacon Fan Club this is another excuse to use it and a way of preventing turkey or chicken from drying out. Lay some strips of bacon over the bird. The fat from the bacon bastes the meat while it's cooking. You can do this for pieces or for a whole bird. Great when roasting and grilling.

Rubbing the bird with butter before cooking is also a form of light barding.

A pork-based stuffing will work on the same theory for the inside of the chicken or turkey, just don't forget to adjust the cooking time for the weight of the stuffing.

Brining

This keeps a turkey moist through its long roasting process, but you can brine chickens too. When you brine a bird you submerge it in a salt-water solution. The brine soaks into the bird and the moisture remains in the flesh during roasting, making it unlikely to dry out, but leaving a nice crispy brown skin. The salt, a natural tenderiser, keeps the meat from toughening. It is a win win situation.

A basic brine is 225g of salt to 4 litres of water with an optional 225g of sugar. And while you are at it, why not throw in some brown sugar, maple syrup, honey or molasses in place of the sugar, bay leaves, juniper berries, mustard seed, fennel seed, caraway seed, cloves of crushed garlic, onions, allspice berries, cinnamon stick, fresh sage, cider, beer, vinegar, mirin, wine, rice wine vinegar, orange or other fruit juice, soy sauce, ginger, stock, tea or espresso. Submerge the bird completely in the brine, and keep it somewhere cold – preferably the refrigerator, but some people have been known to keep turkeys in buckets of brine outside in the winter, if they don't fit in the fridge. After brining, pat dry, allow to come up to room temperature and roast.

Buttermilk or yoghurt brine/marinade

If you are going to deep-fry chicken or turkey may whatever saint there is of fried birds forgive you if you skip the buttermilk marinade. They are also wonderful for roast or grilled chicken pieces and are very popular in Indian cooking before braising or roasting. Both tenderise and brine in a creamy way.

Choose from any of these spices or a combination: garlic, toasted cumin or coriander seeds, jalapeno, chilli powder, paprika, onion, basil, shallot, parsley, mint, honey, citrus juice or zest, mustard, garam masala, ginger.

Brining times

Whole chicken: 6–12 hours
Chicken or turkey pieces: 1–3 hours
Whole turkey: 24–48 hours

Great ways to stuff a bird

- Stuff loosely because stuffing expands.

- About 1 kilo of stuffing will fill the average-sized turkey.

- Add the weight of the stuffing to the weight of the bird. If you forgot to weigh the stuffing, have someone stand on the bathroom scales, then hand them the stuffed bird and subtract their weight from the total.

- You can also cook the stuffing completely separately. This will reduce the weight and therefore the cooking time so there will be less drying out of the bird. It will also reduce any hygiene risks (see below). Roll the stuffing into balls and bake at 190°C/gas mark 5 for about half an hour until they're golden brown.

Stuffing can be dangerous:

- Allow the stuffing to cool completely prior to putting it in the bird and always stuff the bird just before roasting. If you let it sit around raw with warm stuffing in it, it may develop bacteria.

- Remove the stuffing as you are carving. Don't refrigerate the leftover bird with the stuffing still in it because it keeps the heat in, and you may wind up with a bird stuffed with a breeding ground for bacteria.

Easy peasy sausage stuffing

Start by making breadcrumbs from about 4–5 thick slices of bread. You can experiment with the type of bread you use: corn, rye and sour dough are all good choices. Then you need 225g sausage meat, salt and pepper and beaten eggs. Add a selection from the following: grated zest and juice of a lemon, a chopped onion or shallots fried in butter, thyme, sage, parsley, chopped chestnuts, dried apricots, sultanas, port-soaked dried cranberries, raisins, bacon, celery sautéed in butter, apricots, apples, pecans, dried plums, Armagnac-soaked plums, dried figs, or dried figs soaked in vermouth.

Stuffing under the skin

Up the flavour quotient when roasting, grilling or braising a whole bird or pieces by gently lifting the skin round the breast from the flesh. Leave the skin intact and try not to poke holes in it. Then stuff it with pesto, regular stuffing, herbs, butter mixed with herbs, diced fruit or mixtures of anything you think might add flavour. If you are using a more hearty bread-based stuffing between the skin and the breast, it increases the overall breast thickness, so it takes longer to cook but keeps the breast moist while the legs get done. Cook according to the finished weight of the bird and stuffing.

A very special skill

When chickens hatch, they are separated by sex. The person who does this job is called a chicken sexer and the good ones can determine the sex of 80,000 chicks a day with almost 100 per cent accuracy.

Roasting

- Always remove the fowl from the fridge with enough time for it to come to room temperature before cooking it.

- Always clean a bird inside and out before stuffing and roasting (dry with kitchen paper).

- Carry out any or a combination of the above methods for preparation.

- To check if it's done, test the thickest part, the juice should run clear. Don't mess around with poultry; never serve it undercooked.

- Remove the bird from the heat, baste just once and let it rest for 15 minutes before serving. Use the juice for gravy or sauce.

- One unstuffed roast chicken serves 2 to 4 people.

- Roasting times:
  - Chicken: 20 minutes per 450g plus additional 20 minutes at 180°C/gas mark 4 for birds up to 4 kilos, for larger birds add a further 15 minutes per 450g. Add 5 minutes per pound if the bird is stuffed.
  - Duck: 20 minutes per 450g at 180°C/gas mark 4. Start with the oven at 230°C/gas mark 8 for 5 minutes, then turn it down to 180°C/gas mark 4. This will help give a crispier skin. Although it can be served rare, unlike chicken, you still want to make sure the juices are running clear.
  - Turkey: 15 minutes for every 450g plus 5 extra minutes per 450g if stuffed. Start with 15 minutes at 220°C/gas mark 7 then lower the heat to 180°C/gas mark 4. Baste it every 30 minutes.
  - Goose: 15 minutes for every 450g plus 15 minutes. Start with 30 minutes at 230°C/gas mark 8 then lower the heat to 190°C/gas mark 5 for the remainder of the time. Some people parboil their goose for 30 minutes before roasting, this will cut the amount of fat that runs off during cooking.

- Always let the meat rest after cooking. A chicken will need about 10 to 20 minutes, a larger bird will need more. If you want, you can try turning the bird upside down while it is resting. The theory is that more of the liquid will run into the breast meat, making it juicier.

Some tips from Caroline

- Some people like to roast the bird on all sides. Start it on the breast side then flip it onto its side, then the other side, then onto its back. Other people feel the breast meat shouldn't ever touch the pan bottom, because it overcooks so easily anyway, and also it's a bit of a pain to keep turning it over. Try it both ways and see which one you like best.

- Roasting a bird with a lard-covered cloth reduces the likelihood of uneven cooking between the breast and the thighs. In a way it is a form of barding.

- Roasting a chicken in the same pan as root vegetables or autumn fruits makes a great one-pot meal.

- Mid-flight-gravy-making technique: make a roux with the chicken fat by sprinkling the bird with flour halfway through cooking. Let it cook for 5 minutes, then baste frequently.

- Adding a glaze: 15–20 minutes before the bird has finished roasting, brush it with preserves, honey, barbecue sauce, sweet chilli sauce or anything else you like (optionally mixed with some butter). Wait 5–10 minutes. Repeat. Repeat.

Pan frying

This is the perfect preparation for making gravy with afterwards. Cook using skin on, bone-in pieces of chicken and only with very tender birds. Over a medium heat, cook for 30 minutes, moving and flipping the pieces round frequently for even cooking. You can finish off in the oven at 180°C/gas mark 4 for the last 10 minutes to assure a more even finish and to crisp up the skin. If you are using fillets start with the flesh-side down, for the first half, then finish with the skin-side down. Don't rush by using a high heat – if you need to hurry, cover the pan for the first half and don't overcook or it will dry out and toughen.

Stir frying

As simple as chopping, slicing or dicing some turkey, chicken or duck and cooking it over high heat in some fat. Chicken breast tends to sweat, so allow the liquid to cook off.

· A TIP FROM LARA ·

Next time you do a stir fry, or any dish you could use strips of chicken breast for, try using chicken thighs instead. They are much less expensive and don't dry out nearly as easily. The end dish is cheaper and has stronger flavour and texture.

Deep frying

A vat of boiling fat might be something you like to avoid over a hot flame in your kitchen. Maybe this is why fried chicken is one of the most popular takeaways – because no one wants to make it at home. But do try it. It is easy, takes less actual cooking time than roasting and man, does it taste good. Replacing portions of frying oil with rendered bacon, chicken or duck fat adds to extra heart-doctor-shocking goodness.

One chicken cut into 8 pieces serves 4–6:

- Marinade in ½ litre of buttermilk with a diced onion, salt and cayenne pepper overnight in the fridge. Do not skip this step. It is what makes it good.

- Spice 500g of flour with any of these: ground black pepper, white pepper, paprika, cayenne, cumin, salt, pinch of dried mustard. Anything that sounds good to you. Combine well.

- Remove the chicken from the buttermilk and dredge with the flour then let it sit for 20 minutes.

- Heat 1 litre of oil to 180ºC. At that temperature it will take 40 seconds for a bread cube to brown. Don't cook more than 3 or 4 pieces at a time otherwise you run the risk of lowering the oil temperature and ending up with soggy under-cooked chicken. Cook chunks, strips, breast and wings for about 10 minutes, 12 minutes for drumsticks and thighs.

- Drain on paper towels and serve hot or cold.

Cooking times for grilling

Kebabs: 10 minutes

Skinless boneless breasts: 7 minutes per side depending on thickness

Skinless boneless thighs: 5 minutes per side

Quartered chicken: 30 minutes total, turn over halfway through so it cooks evenly

Bone-in skin-on breast: 20–25 minutes total, turn over halfway through so it cooks evenly

For just the wings: 8–10 minutes per side

Spatchcocked: 20–30 minutes

Steaming and poaching

These are very good low fat, low cholesterol ways of cooking chicken. It doesn't require any pre-treating (marinades or rubs), but benefits hugely from just about any sauce that goes with poultry.

1. Brown the bird first in oil for extra flavour, if you like.

2. Poach for an hour for a whole chicken, 30 to 40 minutes for pieces.

3. If you want to use the liquid for a sauce, reduce it by at least half first.

Braising, stewing, casseroling, pot roasting or slow cooking

No need to marinade, stuff, rub or tie with this method, just brown and throw it in a pot with anything you think it might be tasty with. Use pieces with or without the skin, but braising with the bone in improves flavour. Braised poultry almost always tastes better the next day, making for great leftovers and the perfect pot-luck dish. Traditionally speaking, casseroling, braising and pot roasting happened in the oven while stewing was done on the hob. These days these terms have become fairly interchangeable. Casseroling and braising recipes generally use pieces of poultry, whereas pot roasting is always done with a whole bird (or a joint of meat), which is at least partially covered with vegetables and liquid – sort of a combination of roasting and casseroling. Don't try to pot roast a whole duck or goose, they are way too fatty, nor turkey either, it's too large.

1. Heat a large deep ovenproof casserole dish with a lid to a medium temperature. Brown the bird in some oil.

2. Remove bird and keep to the side. Add some aromatic vegetables like diced onions, carrots and celery to the casserole to make a flavour base.

3. When the vegetables start to brown, deglaze the pan with stock, wine, juices, tomato sauce..

4. Return the bird to the casserole dish. Add any other ingredients (see suggestions below), cover and bake at 180°C/gas mark 4 for ½ to 1½ hours depending on the size of the bird.

5. Check the liquid level from time to time so it doesn't dry up.

6. Let it rest and give it time for the flavours to marry. Finish off with a sprinkling of fresh herbs, chopped nuts, bread-crumbs or even diced fruit.

Good flavour combinations

Brine-cured black olives, broad beans, chillies, chorizo, cider, corn, cream, currants, garlic, herbs de Provence, hot sauce, leeks, mustard, red cabbage, rosemary, saffron, salsa, stock, sweet potato, tomatoes, thyme, white wine.

Chicken facts

If you have a paralysing fear of chickens, you are an alektorophobe or, to use common nomenclature, a chicken.

Ways to tell when the bird is done

- To check a turkey pierce the thickest part of the crown, the juice should run golden or clear. If pink, cook for 10–15 minutes more, then test again.

- To test most other birds, do the same, but pierce the bird closer to where the thigh meets the back. Basically, you want to check the thickest part, and usually you want to test the dark meat, because it cooks more slowly.

- Another test, though not as reliable as the juices running clear, is to pull on a leg, there should be some give if it's done. Sometimes it will even pop right out of the socket.

- Then there is the stick-a-meat-thermometer-in-it method. It is cooked when the internal temperature is 75°C. Take care to check the thickest portion and don't have the thermometer touching any bone. Duck breast should not exceed an internal temperature of 57°C. Easy to remember: whole birds done at 75°C, switch the numbers round for duck breast.

Carve it up

Chicken and turkey

The bird should be breast-side up. Use a long thin sharp knife as opposed to a butcher's knife for slicing, and use one of those large carving forks to help you keep it in place. First remove the drumstick and thigh from one side, then the wing on that side, then the breast. Repeat on the other side. Then divide the drumstick from the thigh.

Duck

Turn the duck onto its breast, cut all the way down the back on both sides of the backbone. Open it out like a book and cut through the breastbone so you have two parts. Lay one half on its back and cut the meat away, starting from the top and keeping the knife close to the bone. When you get to the bottom, you want to cut through the leg joint and take the whole leg away with the breast. Repeat this with the other side. You should have two big pieces. Cut between the leg and breast of each half, so you have four pieces then cut each of those pieces in half, cutting the leg at the joint and the breast in half.

In some Chinese restaurants, they don't bother to carve it. They use a cleaver and, starting with the still intact head end, the bird is hacked into strips down to the tail.

· A TIP FROM CAROLINE ·

Use the resting juices from the carving board. Even if you are not making gravy, pour them over the sliced meat.

Chicken facts

Egyptians cultivated chickens 4,000 years ago and built enormous incubators that could hold 10,000 chicks. For anyone who has been in near proximity to just a dozen chicks in an incubator, imagine the noise that must have made!

Portion calculator

- Ducks don't have as much meat as chickens: one large duck will feed 4 people.

- Christmas turkey: 500 to 750g per person. The perfect size for a turkey is 5.4–6.3 kilos; anything bigger then 9 kilos will not be as flavourful, you'd be better off getting two small ones.

File under conversation piece

Beer Can Chicken

This is only for outdoor grills that have covers and are big enough to fit a chicken, standing up.

    1 chicken prepared as you would for roasting (rubs or
        marinades optional) salted inside and out
    1 can beer

Trim off excess fat. Heat the grill to medium.

With a can opener, make 5 holes in the top of the beer can.

Insert the beer can into cavity of the chicken and stand it up on the grill.

Cook it for 2 hours with the grill covered. The beer will baste the chicken from the inside as it cooks. Remove from the grill, remove the beer can with possibly very hot beer still in it.

Let it rest for 15 minutes, serve.

Chapter seven

·

Meat

Almost every creature and plant that doesn't actually
poison us has, at some moment or other, become part of
the human diet.

RIVER COTTAGE FAMILY COOKBOOK

One of us was a vegetarian for most of her younger
years, and the other is very interested in vegan cooking, so cooking meat was a big part of our year-long
challenge. For Lara (the former vegetarian) the key was over-
coming her fear and intimidation and for Caroline (the vegan
friendly) the question was how to make it interesting enough
to be worthwhile. A year later Lara is fearless and cooking
meat on a regular basis, and Caroline has become a star at
cooking offal in new and experimental ways. We have both
found our own way to love the meat cooking process.

Meat speak

- Hanging: after an animal has been slaughtered the meat is left to hang from a couple of days to 6 weeks depending on the amount of fat that covers the meat. It makes the texture of the meat softer and the flavour better because moisture evaporates from the muscle for a greater concentration of flavour, and the meat enzymes break down and make it more tender.

- Halal and kosher: animals are raised and slaughtered in accordance with religious codes.

- Marbling: refers to thin lines of fat running through the meat. Fat = flavour, and the more marbling the better the cut of meat.

- Skimming: to tilt the pan and spoon most of the fat off. You can get a little more off by using kitchen paper.

- Rare breed: this does not mean endangered, it just means that it is an old or prestigious breed, like Aberdeen Angus or Wagyu beef. Prime beef means it comes from a pedigree herd.

Offal is not awful

Offal comes from the phrase 'off fall'. When a carcass is cut open most of the internal organs fall out on to the abattoir floor. Offal includes heart, liver, kidney, tongue, brain, testicles, lungs, sweetbreads (the thymus or pancreas gland of lamb or calf), tripe and blood, also pig's trotters, head and cheek, oxtail, and calves' feet.

Most offal is made from fibrous and otherwise unappealing material that must be, depending on what it is, soaked, scraped, pressed, peeled, boiled or deveined before you can cook it. Using offal and taking the time to make it into something that tastes good is admirable and the results worthwhile. Sometimes the preparation process can take a couple of days, so always start the day you buy it.

Better than the hair of the dog?

Tripe is something of a universal hangover cure, finding its way into weekend morning stews like *menudo* in Mexico and *iskembe corbasi* in Turkey.

How to tell if you've found a good butcher

- Whether you want chops, cubes, a guard of honour, or a boned-out leg, the butcher should happily do it for you. Some preparations are very hard to do without the right tools and experience.

- If you want a special kind or cut of meat, or a certain kind of offal they don't have in stock a good butcher will try to order it.

- A butcher should make suggestions telling you what's good today, or how to cook whatever looks good to you.

- A good butcher doesn't look at you like a deer in the headlights when you ask for a less common cut of meat or offal.

Five steps to choosing good meat on your own

1. Make sure the meat doesn't smell sweaty. That's true of most things. Some meat that has been hung for a long time may develop a gamy smell but, other than that, strong smells are a bad sign.

2. Avoid too much blood. Meat that looks wet with blood, or beef or lamb that are bright red, have not been hung properly, and will be tough and tasteless. Also avoid meat with a pink/brown two-tone appearance. It's bad news.

3. Check the fat. You're looking for a good creamy layer. Yellow or grey fat or, in the case of pork a rubbery rind, are all signs that you should stay clear.

4. Make sure the meat is shiny, firm and tacky to the touch. Beef should be a dark rich red, or even purplish in some cases. Lamb will be a lighter colour than beef, but you want a good matt red; pork should be pale pink, smooth and fine grained.

5. Be sure the shop is clean and the food is laid out with care. If the food has just been thrown anyhow into the display case, it doesn't say much for the care they take.

Keep it fresh

If you are buying meat pre-packed from the supermarket it will have a use-by date on it. Never cook anything that has passed this date. If you are buying it from a butcher, or farmers' market, then the general rule is: don't keep fresh meat in the fridge for longer then two days. If you are freezing meat, freeze it before its use-by date. Do not refreeze meat unless you have cooked it, then you can refreeze the fully cooked and completely cooled dish.

Portion calculator

These portions are suggested for dinner for adults and are per person:

1–2 pork chops

2–4 lamb chops

500g for very bony cuts, like ribs

150g of boneless cuts

225g for bone in cuts

Double this for the holidays!

Love me tender

Tenderising can make the difference between a tough inedible disaster, and a gorgeous dinner you will enjoy and be proud of. When deciding on your method, think about the cut of meat you are using. Does it just need a little nudge or does it need the full treatment? It's safe to say that the parts of the animal that did the least work are going to be the most tender, better suited to fast cooking and light tenderising. The parts that worked hard every day will be tougher and taste better if slow cooked and with more serious forms of tenderisation. Here are the different methods we've used over our year-long experiment:

- Pounding: hooray for an excuse to use the meat mallet! If you don't have one, a rolling pin will do. Coolest stand-in for the meat mallet is the side of a cleaver if you are hard core enough to have one of those. Pounding breaks up tough fibres in the meat and tenderises it. If you like, pound the meat between two sheets of wax paper or parchment. This keeps the meat in place and prevents it from splattering. Optional for cuts that are going to be sautéed or pan fried.

- Scoring: a good trick for meat that is extra tough. It also boosts the effect of a marinade. Make shallow cuts in one direction, then again at 45° angles. This should make a diamond pattern. Do both sides of the meat.

- Brining: good for any section of the animal: chops, loin and tenderloin, particularly of pork, all benefit greatly, and larger joints can be transformed by it. German Sauerbraten and Irish corned beef are both larger cuts of meat that have been brined for a long time before cooking. See page 107 for more information.

- Larding: sewing strips of fat through the meat using a larding needle, or pressing it into incisions made with a sharp knife. This is done with leaner cuts of meat like tenderloin. You can also stick in cloves of garlic, branches of rosemary or anything else that goes with meat.

- Barding: wrapping or covering the meat in sheets of fat, usually bacon fat. This is especially good for venison because it is a very lean meat and dries out easily. It's also very useful for smaller cuts of pork. Boneless chops like to be barded too.

- Marinades: both wet and dry will help tenderise and can do wonders for flavour. Use 125ml of marinade for every 500g of meat. Marinade a piece of meat just long enough to add a little flavour, or it could be more utilitarian: wet marinades always contain acid and salt which help tenderise the meat. A cut of meat marinated for 12 hours or more will have a cooking time about ⅔ the length it would be if cooked with no marinating.

> ### *Strange fruit*
>
> A now defunct method of tenderising meat was to inject the animals with papain, a papaya derivative before they were slaughtered

Making it taste good

Dry rubs

These are basically dry marinades. Use about 75g of dry rub per 500g of meat. Apply it about 30 minutes before cooking.

- Beef spices: basil, chillies, coriander (fresh and seeds), cumin, garlic, horseradish, mustard (dried or prepared), pepper (black and white).

- Pork spices: cayenne, coriander, cumin, fennel, garlic, mustard, onion powder, paprika, pepper (black and white), rosemary, sage, star anise, sugar (white or brown).

- Lamb spices: cloves, cumin, curry, dill, dried mint, garlic, mustard, oregano, rosemary.

Wet marinades

Use any of the above spices, and . . .

- For beef: ale or stout, balsamic vinegar, bay, capers, chives, green peppercorns, honey, horseradish, mirin, olive oil, onions, orange (juice, zest, peel), parsley, spring onions, red wine, shallots, soy sauce, vinaigrette.

- For pork: apples, bay, beer, brandy, cider vinegar, coriander, hoi sin sauce, honey, mangos, maple syrup, mint, molasses, mustard, onions, orange juice, parsley, pineapple, soy sauce, white wine.

- For lamb: capers, fresh mint, honey, lemon zest, olive oil, pomegranate juice, redcurrant jelly, red wine, soy sauce, tamarind, yoghurt.

Three other ways to make it taste good

1. Salsa verde

Salty but fresh tasting, this strong combination of flavours tends to work well with other strongly flavoured foods from oily fish to lamb. It's really easy to make too.

1 clove of garlic
2 anchovies
1–2 tablespoons capers, drained and rinsed
juice of ½ lemon
handful of flat-leaf parsley
60ml olive oil (more if needed)

Chop everything really fine, and then basically just mash it using as much of the olive oil as you need to make a paste. This can be added before cooking, or after. Some other wonderful additions are: mustard (prepared or powder), fresh basil, fresh mint, chopped hard-boiled egg, breadcrumbs, red wine vinegar.

2. Chimichurri

From Argentina, this is a fresh and spicy topping or marinade for meats.

MAKES ABOUT 240ml
1 bunch of flat-leaf parsley, chopped
100ml extra virgin olive oil
1 teaspoon hot pepper flakes
3 cloves of garlic, chopped
½ teaspoon salt
45ml red wine vinegar or fresh lemon juice
ground black pepper

Mix all the ingredients together, let it sit so the flavours marry for 30 minutes then spoon it over meat or chicken.

3. Gremolata

This is like chimichurri's Italian little sister.

2 tablespoons flat-leafed parsley, chopped finely
1 garlic clove, mince
1 teaspoon lemon zest

Mix together and sprinkle over meat, potatoes and vegetables.

Ways to get the stuffing in

Preparing cuts of meat for stuffing at home is possible, but very difficult unless you have really good knives, and knife skills. Each method is useful for specific types of cooking. This is the sort of thing your butcher should do for you.

- Boning and rolling: first they remove the bone, then roll up the cut of meat and secure it with butcher's string. This is a classic roasting joint. To stuff it just cut off the strings, unroll the meat, slather it with whatever flavours you like, roll it back up and retie it. This is great with traditional stuffings and also with wonderful flavour enhancers like gremolata in a pork roast, or salsa verde with lamb.

- Tunnel boning: the bone of a leg of lamb is removed without cutting the meat, so it leaves a little tunnel that can be stuffed for roasting. These joints are wonderful for holiday meals; they look very festive, like a cornucopia. You can stuff them with a classic stuffing, or try a bread- or rice-based stuffing with sultanas and pine nuts. Because the leg is left whole, when you slice it you will have a ring of meat round a circle of stuffing.

- Butterflying a leg of lamb: like boning and rolling, only they don't always roll it. It is specific to legs of lamb. Any bones are removed and then the meat is cut so you can open it out like a book. Making it flat like this makes it very easy to wrap it round some stuffing and secure it with string.

- Guard of honour: rack of lamb which you often see in fancy magazines. First they take two racks of rib chops (each is one piece containing several rib chops) and expose the thin ends of the bones by scraping off any meat or fat. Then they are pressed together so the exposed rib bones interlock and are secured with string. Some people also add little paper decorations to the ends of the bones. Next you roast it. If you want, you can stuff the gap in-between the two racks. Whether you do or not, this is one of the most elegant presentations of a roast.

Before you start cooking

- Quick methods of cooking, like pan frying and grilling, are for tender cuts of meat only.

- Slow cooking, like pot roasting and casseroling are great for tougher cuts, it gives them a chance to soften up and fully develop their flavour.

- Make sure the meat is at room temperature before you cook it. This will give a more consistent cooking time, and help with an even cooking.

- Make sure you always wipe a piece of meat dry before browning or searing it.

Choose a method, avoid the madness

Roasting

Best for:

lamb: leg and shoulder, whole loin, saddle, rack, or best end

beef: sirloin, rib joint, wing rib, back rib

pork: leg, loin, spare rib, tenderloin, belly

Lara's tips on oven roasting

- For the best results, roast the meat fat-side up on a wire rack or a bed of vegetables. That way the fat will drip away, basting the meat as it goes.

- If you are roasting a boned pork loin use the bones as a roasting rack to add flavour to the gravy.

- Place a small halved onion underneath the roast. It will caramelise and help make great gravy.

- Generally, you should baste two or three times while roasting, but if you are roasting pork, don't baste over the crackling or it won't crisp.

- Don't forget to check the pan juices once in a while. If they dry up, it will ruin the gravy, and possibly your pan. If you have too much liquid at the end, it can always be reduced before you use it.

Three things you need to know about crackling

1. Make sure the roasting tin isn't too deep; the meat has to have good exposure to the heat.

2. Make sure the skin is dry and salted. Do not use oil on the skin. It needs to be dry in order to crisp up.

3. Accept the fact that sometimes it just doesn't crisp. There will always be a next time.

Pan roasting

If the cut of meat is too thick to fry but too small to roast, brown it in a pan first and then put it into the oven to finish it off.

Fast cooking (frying or grilling)

Best for:

lamb: cutlets, loin chops, whole loin, brochettes, leg steaks, chump chops, noisettes

beef: fillet or tenderloin, sirloin steak, rump steak, t-bone steak, rib-eye steak

pork: fillet, tenderloin, chops, escallops, leg steaks, bacon

Caroline's tips on grilling

- Sear the heck out of a steak at high heat to keep the juices in, then finish cooking it at a lower heat to give you more control of the final result – rare, medium or well done.

- Though you have fewer sauce possibilities with grilling, you can make marinades that can go on before, during or afterwards. This is also a perfect occasion to use up frozen sauces that have been waiting in the freezer. Even without a sauce, a nice grilled piece of meat is good on its own, hot or cold.

- You can start a piece of meat under the grill then put it in the oven for a more even finish.

- Because the heat of a grill can be inconsistent you need to move the meat around constantly and keep checking for doneness so it cooks evenly.

- Brush the meat not the rack with oil.

- If you are using charcoal, wait till the flames go down and the coals are white on the outside, glowing red inside.

Caroline's tips on frying

- Use a pan with a heavy base for even heat distribution, and don't overcrowd the pan or the meat will boil rather than fry.

- Get the pan as hot as possible, then add the oil and when it is just about smoking you are ready to go.

- Sear the meat for a minute on each side, before turning down the heat for the remainder of the cooking time. This will seal the meat and keep more of the juices inside.

- When the meat's done, remove it to a plate so you can deglaze the pan and make a sauce or gravy (see pan sauce on page 30).

- Pan frying apples, pineapples, bananas, or stone fruits, like plums, makes a good side dish for pork and game.

Slow cooking

Best for any meat labelled 'braising' or stewing, also:

lamb: breast, shin, neck, or any cut of mutton

beef: forequarter meat (chuck or blade), shoulder, skirt, top rump, topside, oxtail, rump, leg, hock, shin, silverside, top-side, short rib, brisket

pork: bacon joint, gammon shoulder, knuckle of bacon

Slow cooking includes casseroling, braising, stewing, pot roasting and boiling. Some people shy away from slow cooking because it takes so long, but the beauty of it is that the majority of the time there is very little preparation involved, and you won't have to do anything at all during the actual cooking. These recipes are the perfect thing for a Sunday at home. You put it in, forget about it, go about your business, and then by dinner time, there is this amazing meal. It is also a great way to use a cheaper cut of meat and turn it into something really luxurious.

Lara's tips on slow-cooking

- All slow-cooking methods involve a substantial amount of cooking liquid, and the meat should be partly if not entirely submerged.

- Unless you're boiling, avoid using water as the liquid, you'll do much better with wine, stock, cider or whatever marinade you may have used for the meat.

- Make sure the food is simmering when it goes into the oven. With the oven so low, if it isn't simmering, a good amount of cooking time will be spent just getting the food up to the right temperature.

- If you are slow cooking on the hob, make sure you have the heat very low. Check occasionally to make sure it is just simmering and, for some recipes, you'll have to top up the liquid periodically.

- Slow-cooked dishes are often better the next day. You can cool it, and then leave it in the fridge. This also makes it really easy to remove the fat because it will solidify on top and you can just scrape it off before reheating.

- To reheat a casserole or braised dish, a good guideline is to heat the oven to 180ºC/gas mark 4 and cook for 35 to 45 minutes. Make sure the liquid comes to a simmer. If you have frozen the casserole, make sure it is fully thawed before reheating it.

- When boiling, don't forget to skim regularly to remove any scum that rises to the top.

How to tell when it's done

BEEF

	Rare	Medium	Well
Desired internal temperature **	46–54°C	54–66°C	66–71°C
Fry and grill 2-cm thick steak	1½–2 mins each side	2½–3 mins each side	3½–4 mins each side
Fry and grill 3-cm thick steak	4 mins each side	5 mins each side	6 mins each side

LAMB

	Rare	Medium	Well
Desired internal temperature **	60°C	65°C	70°C
Fry and grill lamb chops		10 mins	
Fry and grill lamb cutlets		8 mins	

PORK

	Rare	Medium	Well
Desired internal temperature **	57°C	68°C	78°C+ is overcooked
Fry and grill pork chops		10 mins	

* Times assume the meat is always brought to room temperature before cooking and has been seared at a very high temperature first.

** This is for all cuts of meat and all methods of cooking

The touch test

You can tell when a grilled or pan-fried steak or chop is done by pressing on it. This method is one of those things that, if you can do it, makes you look like a really accomplished chef. Firstly because you are tough enough to press your finger on a hot piece of meat without letting the heat get to you and secondly it makes you appear as though you have an almost physic connection with the meat and it is talking to you through your fingertips.

- underdone: soft and mushy

- rare: soft with some bounce

- medium rare: soft but springs back

- medium: hard and springy

- well done: very firm with little spring

Meat needs its rest

Don't go directly from pan to plate. Let all meat rest for 5 to 15 minutes. Smaller cuts need less time, larger ones need longer. Resting meat after it cooks makes it tender and juicy. As the juices heat up they begin to move towards the surface like water bubbling up. Giving the meat time to relax gives the juices time to seep back into the meat.

Chine up

If you have trouble carving, you can have your roasting joint chined. This means the butcher loosens the bone in a joint, but leaves it attached. That way you get all the roasting benefit of the bone being in, but once the joint is cooked, you can remove the bone for easy carving. Don't try to chine it at home; it's better left to the professionals.

When you need to cook the whole cow

Closed-Pit Barbecued Beef

Serves 500 to 1,000

Butcher a cow and split the carcass in half or into smaller more manageable sections if you aren't man enough to flip a whole half a cow. Dig a large pit approx. 3 metres across, 4 metres wide and 1½ metres deep. Erect metal netting to form a grill over the pit strong enough to support 1 ton. Fill the pit with wood, light it and let it burn to coals. Place the beef on the grill, turning it often with a pitchfork. Using a cotton mop, regularly slather the meat with barbecue sauce (types vary according to local preference). Serve with beer.

Chapter eight

·

Food from the Sea

It was the Law of the Sea, they said. Civilization ends at the waterline. Beyond that, we all enter the food chain, and not always right at the top.

HUNTER S. THOMPSON, American author and journalist (1937–2005)

The first American edition of *Larousse Gastronomique* explains, 'The most nourishing fish are river eels and lampreys, then come salmon, salmon trout, mackerel, turbot, fresh herring and the conger eel. Among the least nourishing, although they are by no means to be despised are bream, sole and lemon sole.'

Fish are dangerous

Fish and shellfish present the most immediate health hazards of all the proteins from bacteria, parasites, viruses, pollutants and toxins. Seafood can turn bad faster than any other food we regularly eat. Fish are cold blooded and their flesh is used to existing in a cold aquatic environment. The bacteria that live on and in fish are also used to thriving in the cold which could either be cold water or your fridge. The usual temperature of a fridge – 1.5–5°C is the same temperature these spoilage bacteria do their best work.

Fish are less dangerous than coconuts

Annual deaths from ingestion
of the deadly fugu or puffer fish   approx. 50

Annual deaths from shark attack   approx. 15

Annual deaths caused by falling coconuts   approx. 150

But still, some fish are quite scary

- The candirü fish is a very small Amazonian catfish that has the ability to swim up a stream of urine and lodge in your urethra.

- In very rare cases, certain coral-reef fish carry toxins called *gambierdiscus toxicus*. It collects in the liver of the fish. If exposed to it, among the many symptoms that can be experienced is something called sensory inversion, which means that hot things will feel cold and cold things will seem hot.

Fish are awesome

Fish are rich in omega 3 fatty acids, which help limit the inflammatory responses of the body, and as a result lower the incidence of heart disease and cancer. People living in cultures with more fish in their diet tend to live longer.

Buying fish and shellfish

Top five reasons to go to a fishmonger

1. They know what the best fish of the day is – fish have seasons just like fruit and vegetables do. Seafood in season will generally be the best.

2. They can tell you what fish can be used as a substitute if your fish choice is out of season or otherwise unavailable.

3. They will scale, bone and skin the fish for you – removing the most worrying part of fish preparation. It is not uncommon for them to weight the fish before cleaning it and charge you the pre-cleaned fish price.

4. They can tell you how to cook the fish too – if something looks good but you don't know what to do with it, just ask. They'll know a great way to prepare it. Also, don't be afraid to ask someone who is buying a fish you are interested in what they plan on doing with it.

5. They know when and where your fish came from. By the time a fish gets to a supermarket, it has probably had to go to a distribution centre and then off to the individual shop, meaning it has been in transit for several days. Sometimes your fishmonger can get you a fish that was swimming the day before.

How to pick a good fishmonger

- A good fish shop should smell like the sea. People make jokes about the smell of fish, but if your fish shop doesn't smell appealing, just keep walking.

- The look of the place should be good and clean and well organised. It should look like everything was laid out with care.

- Last is my secret trick. Tell them what you want to make and that you are a bit low on cash that day. If they still try to sell you the more expensive fish (like a sea bass), they are not being honest with you. All recipes will have a slightly cheaper fish that will work just as well. An honest fish-monger will help you out.

Top five qualities to look for when buying fresh fish

1. Eyes should be clear, not cloudy and not withdrawn into the head.

2. Flesh should be firm.

3. Slime should be clear and present.

4. Smell should be clean.

5. Colours should be clear, gills bright red.

Most fishmongers will keep the fish on ice, which is good, but it should always be kept skin-side down. If the flesh of the fish sits on ice too long it can get frostbite which turns it a bit grey and makes it look kind of cotton-woolly. Then it's no good. Avoid buying fish over the weekend or ordering it in a restaurant on a Sunday. Many fish markets and restaurants don't get deliveries over the weekend. There's a good chance that the fish you come across on a Sunday has been sitting there from Friday and possibly longer.

Portion calculator

Whole small fish	450g
Whole small fish, gutted, head removed	330g
Fish steaks	225g
Fish fillets	150g

Shellfish: how not to lose the oyster lottery

- When buying clams, oysters or mussels they should be alive and healthy. They should be stored on ice and preferably covered. The shell must be unbroken and able to close itself tightly. If you see that one is open, give it a quick tap, and it should close, if not, it's no good.

- If you are buying a pre-cooked lobster or crayfish, and you are not sure about your source, check its tail. If it was cooked alive then its tail will be tightly curled towards it's body. A floppy tail means there is a good chance it was dead when it was cooked, which is bad news.

- Scallops are the only shellfish that don't have to be alive when you buy them fresh.

- Above all: avoid mollusc consumption the day before any important event or while on a date with someone you like and might go home with later that night. Molluscs are a betting person's food: unless from an excellent source you might regret eating them during the next 6–18 hours.

Fish and the internet

If you just can't get good fish locally, or you need something really specific, then you can order it on the Internet and have it shipped to you in a chilled box, usually overnight. Not something you want to do every day, and you have to make sure you have a good source, but it's not bad as a last resort or for a special occasion.

A *few fishy tips*

- Plastic is the enemy of raw fish. Fish needs air. Next time you buy some, as soon as you get it home, wash it gently in cold water, pat it dry with some paper towel, and then put it on a plate with another plate upside down on top of it as a cover. The fish will get enough air to keep it fresh longer, and the top plate will keep the smell from seeping into your fridge .

- To tell if a fish is truly fresh and has never been frozen put it in a bowl of water. If it is fresh it will float.

- Fresh water is the enemy of molluscs such as mussels, clams and oysters. They should be stored on ice, but never allowed to sit in the melted ice water because fresh water will kill them. Bivalves can keep bacteria trapped inside their shell, turning them bad even faster. Never cook and eat a dead mollusc.

- Oysters should be stored cup side down. Every once in a while an oyster will relax its muscles and open up a bit. If its sitting on its side it could lose all it's liquid, which is really important stuff in terms of its own flavour and of flavouring the dish it's being cooked in.

- Always take fish out of the fridge 30 minutes before you want to cook it. If it is an exceptionally hot day, you may only need 15 minutes. This is to get the fish up to room temperature before it goes in the pan or dish to help it to cook more evenly. It's also a good idea to season it with salt when you take it out to improve the texture and boost the flavour, though you shouldn't salt it earlier then 30 minutes or it may dry out.

- These are some saltwater fish: bass, cod, flounder, grouper, haddock, hake, halibut, Atlantic herring, Pacific herring, mackerel, mullet, pilchard, pollock, pompano, red snapper, sea bass, sea trout, shad, the soles, swordfish, tuna, turbot, whiting.

- Here are some freshwater fish: carp, perch, pike, salmon, trout.

- If you decide to eat fish raw, salt cured or gently cold cooked in citrus juice (as in ceviche) do so only with saltwater fish never with freshwater. Freshwater fish contain much more aggressive parasites than saltwater fish and need to be properly cooked.

Preparing fish

Cleaning

If you don't get the fishmonger to prepare the fish for you, here's how to do it yourself:

- Set up: work on 3 layers of newspaper to create a firm work surface so the fish will not slip around so much. Wash the fish and pat dry.

- Scaling: if you are not planning to cook the fish whole, you often don't need to scale it at all and some fish just don't have to be scaled. To test for scales, run the blade of a blunt knife at an almost a 90° angle to the body, from the tail end to the head. If the scales come up easily you have to remove them. Continue running the knife over the fish until the body is smooth and scale free. Remove the top layer of paper containing the scales when you are finished and throw it away. Rinse the fish.

- Gutting: separate the jaw from the throat. Insert the knife into the throat and work the knife towards the tail, stopping at the vent opening by the two fins nearest the tail. The innards, throat and gills should now pull away easily. If not, scoop them out and rinse the fish again. Always remove the gills. They are not edible in any way, shape or form. Even if you are just using the head to make fish stock, the gills have to go.

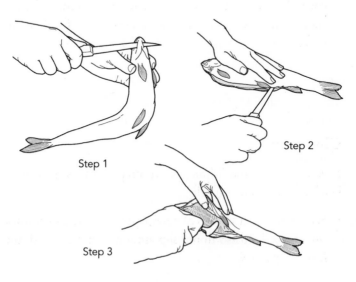

Step 1

Step 2

Step 3

- Optional: leaving the head and bones intact is important for many kinds of fish cookery.

- Beheading: on small fish you should be able to cut straight through, no problem, but for larger fish you'll probably need a big knife. If the bone gives you any problems, either hit it with a rolling pin to help break it, or cut part way through, and then bend the head over the side of the worktop to snap its neck.

- Removing small bones or pin boning: there's not much to say about it other then it's a huge pain. You'll need some needle-nose pliers or some good strong tweezers, then just grab and pull, and try to do as little damage as possible. If you're not sure whether you've got them all, run your finger along the ridge of the fillet, you should be able to feel any you've missed. Seriously, have this done for you if you can.

Filleting

- Round fish: make a cut right down the centre of the back from head to tail, then turn the back towards you. Make another cut, as if you were going to behead the fish, but stop when you hit the bone. Very carefully run the knife (blade parallel to the worktop) just over the bones from the head to the tail. Go gently, a little at a time, pulling the fillet, like a flap, away from the bone, as you go. Repeat on the other side.

- Flat fish: much the same as above but a flat fish has four fillets. Make an incision behind the head and round the outline of the fish. Make another incision straight down the centre of the fish from head to tail and then remove the fillets as above, two from each side.

Steaks

Cut the fish crosswise into sections. If you want to, you can remove or bone the flappy bits from the belly, but for some fish (like salmon) that is a very tasty part. If it's a big fish, you might have trouble cutting through it and you can bash the centre bone a bit with a rolling pin.

Cocktail party fodder

- Liver from the fugu or puffer fish is poisonous and causes almost total paralysis and is a key ingredient in powders used in Haitian zombification rituals. The flesh is a sushi delicacy in Japan. Some claim it will give you a little buzz!

- In Norse mythology when Loki, god of mischief, killed Baldr, god of beauty, he jumped into the river and transformed himself into a salmon in order to escape punishment from the other gods. When they held out a net to trap him he attempted to leap over it but was caught by Thor, who grabbed him by the tail with his hand, which is why the salmon's tail is tapered.

- The salmon of wisdom or the salmon of knowledge is part of an Irish myth. He started out as an ordinary salmon, but then he ate the nuts from the trees surrounding the fountain of wisdom and gained all the knowledge in the world. Eventually he was eaten by Fionn mac Cumhaill and passed on to him all his knowledge, making him a great poet and leader.

- If serving a whole fish always eat the cheeks. Gourmands consider them to be the best part.

- Sometimes you get shellfish that glow in the dark. Next time you buy some, head off to a dark cupboard and check. It's an excellent effect, but means the shellfish is covered with photobacterium and vibrio, a form of ocean algae, so your shellfish isn't at its absolute freshest.

- Lobsters do not age in the same manner as any other creature. In short, their cells do not break down as most other living things do and never reach a point at which the DNA tells them to die. They are also cannibals.

- Before the availability of refrigeration, the Japanese did not consume raw salmon. Salmon and salmon roe have only recently come into use in making sushi.

- Gravlax, a popular Swedish salt-cured salmon that is excellent on bagels with cream cheese or dill sauce, was originally prepared with pine needles instead of dill.

Cooking fish

The number one rule for cooking fish and shellfish is not to overcook it. Unless you are salt baking fish or have an enormous whole fish, you shouldn't go off and have a drink or wash your hair while the fish is cooking although you may certainly pour yourself a drink beforehand and then stand in cat-like readiness for the fish to be perfectly done.

Side dishes that go well with most fish

Artichokes, asparagus, broad beans, broccoli, chips, coleslaw, crêpes, cucumbers, green beans, kale, leeks, pasta, pea greens, peas au bonne femme, potatoes, ratatouille, rice, salad, spinach, tomatoes.

Flavours that go well with most fish

Almond, anchovy, basil, butter, champagne, cider, coriander, cream, cucumber, curry, fennel, gin, guava, horseradish, kiwi fruit, leek, lemon, lime, mace, marjoram, mint, mustard, mushroom, mustard, nutmeg, orange, oyster, rosemary, saffron, tarragon (but not mixed with other herbs), thyme, tomato, vermouth, vodka, white wine.

Pan frying

- Use a non-stick or well-seasoned cast-iron frying pan. Heat it first, then add a little oil (it should come to temperature right away). It will be really hot, so don't worry if there is a little smoke from the oil, but obviously don't burn your house down either.

- Always start cooking fish with the skin-side down. Don't move around or fiddle with it in any way, you'll just break the fillet or pull off the skin.

- Watch it closely because it'll be done pretty quickly. As it begins to cook, it will start to turn opaque from the bottom up. Once it has changed colour, almost up to the top, turn it over, count to 3 and take the pan off the heat.

- Many recipes tell you to pan fry a fillet for a couple of minutes, then flip it over and put the pan in the oven. I don't have a frying pan that can go in my oven or a roasting pan that can go on the hob, so what I do is leave a roasting pan (I like to use glass because of its thickness) in the oven as it preheats. When it comes time to flip the fillet, I flip it right into the preheated dish so it doesn't lose any of the heat going into the oven.

- When shallow frying (or grilling) fish be careful about using butter. It has a great flavour, but can easily burn and ruin the dish. If you want the butter flavour, try using unsalted or clarified butter (ghee) – which will only burn if you really really work hard at it – or, best of all, a mixture of half olive oil and half butter. These compromises will raise the burning point of the butter.

Deep frying

- The oil should be between 180 and 190°C. If you don't have a thermometer, drop in a cube of bread. It should sizzle as soon as it hits the oil and turn brown in under a minute. If the oil isn't hot enough, your food will be greasy and gross, instead of crispy and tasty.

- Don't overcrowd the pan. Too much fish all at once will lower the temperature of the oil. As a matter of fact, it wouldn't hurt to turn the heat up briefly when you first put the fish in, and then turn it back down, to combat the cooling effect of the fish.

- When the batter or coating turns golden brown it is finished. Drain the fish on kitchen towel.

- When doing any kind of crumb or batter coating, make sure you don't coat the fish until it is about to go in the pan to get the best and most even coating. The only exception is egg and crumb coatings, which sometimes need to set. Excellent additions to a dredge-coating can be buckwheat, cornstarch (cornflour), rice flakes, panko (Japanese breadcrumbs), pecans or even crushed plantains.

Fish perfect for deep frying: cod, flounder, grouper, oysters, scallops, clams and turbot.

Poaching

- Add poaching liquid to a sauté pan with a lid – enough so the fish will just be covered – and bring to a simmer before adding the fish. If adding wine, let it simmer for 10 minutes before adding fish.

- Slide the fish into the liquid (fillets go skin-side down), then cover the pan, and simmer for 8 minutes per 2cm of thickness.

- Carefully remove fish from the liquid and drain. The liquid can be made into a sauce or reused the next time you poach.

- Water on its own is never a good medium for poaching. Wine, beer, milk or stock with some herbs, onions or garlic works well. Never let the liquid come to a rolling boil. It should just tremble.

Fish perfect for poaching: sea bass, monkfish, snapper, salmon fillets, lobster, prawns and scallops.

Steaming

You can steam fish in anything, as long as it has a lid and a way to suspend the fish above the water. A conventional steamer, a wok with a rack and lid, a bamboo steamer are all made for just such a task. Adding herbs and flavourings to the water will do nothing for the flavour of the fish, but if you lay the fish on a bed of herbs or something aromatic, it will infuse a subtle flavour. If you lay a towel in-between the fish and the top of the steaming basket (without touching the fish), it will cut down on the amount of condensation that washes over your fish, so the final dish isn't watered down.

Stewing

- Make a soup or stew base in advance, and only add the fish at the very end to prevent overcooking.

- Make sure the liquid covers the fish. Stew until the fish is just cooked through, usually 5 minutes or so will do the trick. If you are stewing larger chunks of fish leave it for about 8 minutes per 2 cm of thickness.

Fish perfect for stewing: shrimp, monkfish, clams, oysters, snapper and scallops.

Grilling indoors and out

- Oil the grilling rack and the fish to help cut down on sticking. Season the fish.

- If grilling outdoors over charcoal, the grill should be 10–12cm above the coals. Continue to oil the fish while it is on the grill.

- Only turn fish once. They are very fragile and can easily fall to pieces if you fiddle too much.

- If you are cooking a fillet with the skin on, grill it skin-side down for almost the entire cooking time. Flip over and remove after 30 seconds.

- A grill basket makes all this much easier. It holds the fish together and prevents it from flaking and breaking apart.

Fish perfect for grilling: sea bass, monkfish, salmon fillets or steaks, lobster (after it has been steamed) tuna steaks, scallops, shrimp, bass, swordfish steaks and flounder.

Microwaving

We're not sure if this is true, but we have heard that God kills a puppy every time someone microwaves a fish, so don't do it. Also, and this we know for a fact, microwaves ruin fish.

Curing and preserving

- Salt curing involves rubbing a filleted fish with a salt and sugar mixture, flavouring it (usually with herbs and maybe spirits), and then weighing it down for 2 to 4 days. To make salmon gravlax, prepare a mixture of 225g sugar, 450g salt and 1 teaspoon of ground white pepper. Put a 450g to 1 kilo extremely fresh salmon fillet with its skin in a glass baking dish. Cover it with the mixture. Sprinkle a large bunch of chopped dill over the fish. Cover and place in fridge for 36 hours, then gently wipe or rinse the fish and discard everything else.

- Ceviche, or seviche is raw fish or shellfish 'cooked' in acid – usually it's lime juice, but you can also use lemon juice or vinegar. When preparing ceviche it is a good idea to freeze the fish for 3 days to kill any parasites. Use 100ml acid per 450g of fish and let it sit for 4 hours or so before serving.

- Escabeche is a pickled fish that is first cooked (usually

lightly fried), and then preserved in a marinade of onions, spices, vinegar and oil. It is similar to ceviche in flavour.

- Soused herrings are stuffed with mustard and dill pickles, and then submerged, uncooked, in a brine made from spices, salt and vinegar.

Baking and roasting

The difference is that roasting generally means you cook something uncovered and in a hotter oven, so baking can be slightly easier because the fish has some protection from the heat. A good temperature for baking fish is anywhere from 180°C to 200°C/gas mark 5 to 6. If you are new to whole fish baking, and apprehensive about it, make 3 or 4 crosswise slashes in each side. This achieves three things:

- It will cut down on the cooking time; less time to stand around worrying.

- It will allow the fish to be infused with more of the flavours of whatever you are cooking it with.

- It will make it easier to check for doneness. If the slashes go down to the bone, then you can just look and see if the colour looks right all the way through.

Fish perfect for roasting: cod, sea bass, monkfish, snapper, salmon fillets and steaks, scallops, swordfish steaks, trout, bass and tuna steaks.

Salt-Baked Whole Fish

You'll need a whole fish, any kind but no smaller than 700g, cleaned with tail, head and scales intact and enough salt to entirely cover the fish – kosher salt works best.

> You need 700g salt to each 450g fish, so a 4-kilo fish can require around 6.5 kilos salt.

Preheat the oven to 200°C/gas mark 6.

Rinse and pat the fish dry. Put a layer of salt on a baking tray large enough to hold the fish. Lay the fish on the salt. If you are planning on stuffing the fish with some extra flavours, now is the time. Put a thin layer of whatever you are using inside its body. Do not overdo it. In this situation, less is more. Entomb the fish in salt. None of the fish should show through the salt. You can't use too much salt; here more is more.

Put it in the oven. A small fish will be done in 20 to 25 minutes. Larger fish will take at least 30 minutes, and you have to test for doneness. See pages 156–7 to check for doneness. Unlike most method of cooking which can leave a fish overdone if you leave it just a few seconds too long, this you can walk away from, have a drink, remember you're cooking something and come back to it. When it's done remove from the heat. Let it cool. With luck you should have a hard thick shell of salt. Crack it when it's cool enough to touch and gently remove it. The fish skin might come off with it; if it doesn't, use a sharp knife to remove it later.

Serve whole, head on, hot or cold, with a sauce.

Braising

The traditional definition of braising is long slow cooking using a bit of liquid, but with fish, long cooking is a relative term. Braising can be done on the hob or in the oven using gentle moderate heat and a covered pan.

- You'll want a bed of vegetables, herbs and/or other flavourful ingredients which you've sautéed. Add enough liquid to come halfway up the fish, but don't go crazy, you don't want to drown it; you just want to keep it from drying out.

- Put the fish in the pan. Cover and simmer, either on the hob or in a preheated 220°C/gas mark 6 oven, until it is tender, about 10 minutes per 2cm of thickness.

Fish perfect for braising: cod, snapper fillets, monkfish, salmon fillets, scallops, trout and flounder.

How to tell when fish and shellfish are done

Cooking times in recipes are at best an educated guess and assume the fish has come to room temperature before cooking. There are many factors that can vary the time needed: the thickness of the fish, a variance of temperature in your pan or oven, how crowded the pan or dish is. If you substitute a different kind of fish in a recipe, it may change the overall cooking time. Here are some general guidelines:

- When cooking a large whole fish, one way to test for doneness is to take a flat metal object, like a knife or skewer. Insert it into the thickest part of the fish, remove and put the knife against your cheek. If it comes out warm, the fish is done.

- Bust out the thermometer, stick it into the thickest part of the fish and hope you haven't let the fish get above 150°C because then it's officially overdone. Best to remove the fish from the heat just as it hits 140°C. This is the minimum cooking temperature which kills bacteria and parasites. The fish will continue to cook even off the heat for a couple more minutes.

- Stick a toothpick into the thickest part of the fish and separate the meat from the bone. The fish is done when the flesh is no longer translucent and flakes easily.

- The best way: the touch test. Takes some time to perfect, but will always work once you have it down pat. Slightly press the fish and if the flesh springs back or returns to its original shape it's done. A variation of this method also works when grilling meat.

- When cooked, bivalves will open up, prawns will turn from translucent to pink.

- Lobster takes about 10 minutes of full-on steaming or boiling to cook.

How to remove fish odour from utensils and your hands
Rub them with lemon juice, vinegar or salt.

How to remove fish odour from sponges or dishcloths
Soak in a solution of 1 teaspoon baking soda to a litre of water.

The Great White Whale Recipe

~

Hardly digestible, far from recommended, and by all accounts undesirable unless you're a sailor from 200 years ago. Still, next time you are in the Arctic Circle and find yourself with a vast hunk of whale:

Allow 225g of whale meat per serving

Whether fresh or frozen soak for 1 hour in a solution of: 1 tablespoon baking soda to a litre of water

Rinse well and marinate for 1 to 2 hours covered in a liquid made up of:

675ml water
225ml vinegar

Cut across the grain into thin steaks not over ½ inch thick.

Sprinkle with lemon juice and pound to tenderise further.

Stew, braise or sauté as for beef, which it resembles more than it does fish, until you think it might be chewable. Serve with riesling.

Chapter nine

·

Bread

Without bread all is misery.

WILLIAM COBBETT, British Journalist (1763–1835)

Bread basics

There are as many different kinds of bakers as there are breads. Some excel at the quick breads. Some labour over loaves for days. For all bakers, there are often more theories than rules. Why some dough behaves the way it does is a point for endless speculation. In one kitchen it will behave one way, in another it may not behave at all. No matter what kind of baker you are or want to become you should:

- Remember that bread baking is mostly about patience and paying huge amounts of attention to what the dough is trying to tell you.

- When it comes to dough you should also remember you can't rush it or ask it to do anything it's not ready to do, and you need to recognise the signs when it is ready.

- Learn to love the process.

One of the perks of baking your own bread is that if you've run out of money by the end of the month, a root vegetable soup and a freshly baked loaf of bread will cost only pennies but feels lavish, comforting and wholesome all at the same time. Another major perk is that baking bread makes your house smell fabulous.

Talk the talk

- Activating: the process of waking up yeast. Yeast starts off in an inactive state (usually dried). You have to activate it by adding liquid.

- Baking or pizza stone: these hold heat very well and give a nicer crust and crumb. An inverted baking sheet will work as a replacement, but will not retain the heat in the same way.

- Cold rise: leaving the dough to rise in the refrigerator. It takes much longer than leaving the dough in a warm place, usually overnight at least.

- Enriched breads: fat, milk, sugar or honey have been added to the dough.

- Enriched flours: vitamins and minerals have been added.

- Flat bread: is as it sounds. Sometimes they are yeast breads, sometimes not, but they will always be rolled or pressed out flat before cooking. Most commonly they are a combination of flour, salt, water and sometimes fats.

- Gluten: the protein of the flour. It turns stretchy and elastic during the kneading process, giving bread its lovely texture. Wheat varieties are called hard, strong or bread if they have a high-gluten content. These are the ones that are easiest to use for bread making. Flours are called soft or weak if the gluten content is low, making them better for cake and pastry making.

- Membrane test: how to tell when bread has been kneaded enough. If you can stretch the dough thin and evenly, creating a membrane that doesn't tear and is translucent, the dough is done kneading.

- Proving/proofing: many breads are left to rise a number of times of various durations before they are baked. Proofing or proving is the last rise before the bread bakes. Usually this takes about an hour.

- Quick breads: generally made from more of a batter than a dough. They rise while baking, and are leavened not with yeast but with baking soda or baking powder and sometimes eggs.

- Rising: allowing the yeast to do its work, doubling the size of your bread dough.

- Scoring: cutting the top of a loaf with a very sharp knife or razor before it is baked. This is done to tame the rise while it bakes and make the loaf pretty as the dough rises, creating what bakers call the bloom.

- Soda bread: a non-yeast bread that rises due to the inter-action of baking soda and lactic acid (usually from buttermilk).

- Soft/elastic: you can stop kneading the dough when it gets to this stage. The texture changes; all of a sudden becoming very smooth and feeling as if it is fighting back a bit. If you poke it with your finger at this point, the indent will start to spring back into shape.

- Knocking/punching down: punching the dough in-between rises to knock the air out. Sometimes you even knead it for a quick minute too.

- Webbing: the pattern of air holes in the bread. Some bread has a very uniform webbing, like quick breads or sandwich breads and others have a varied webbing, like that in a baguette or ciabatta.

- Yeast bread: breads made with yeast; breads that have to rise.

It's in the recipe for a reason

Don't skip the salt or the bread will not rise properly. Salt controls fermentation and strengthens gluten.

The stuff that builds bread

Flour is made from grains, beans, nuts, seeds or sometimes vegetables that have been dried and ground into a powder. Most commonly, flour is made from wheat. The wheat grain is made up of:

- bran: the outer skin of the grain

- germ: the tiny embryo (the part that would sprout)

- endosperm: the starchy white centre (food for the seed)

There are three general types of flour: white flour is made from the endosperm only; whole grain or wholemeal flour is made from the entire grain including bran, endosperm and germ; germ flour is made from the endosperm and germ, excluding the bran.

Lara's favourite bread-related proverbs

Hebrew: buttered bread falls on its face.

Danish: even crumbs are bread.

Polish: he lost his bread and has not found his cake.

Norwegian: first think of bread and then of bride.

Lithuanian: to a starving man bread is sweeter than honey.

Rise up!

If you are making a bread or dough that you want to rise, you need to use a leavener. Most common leaveners are baking soda, baking powder and yeast. Quick breads, cakes and pancakes (among many others) are generally leavened with baking soda and/or baking powder. In some cakes and doughs, eggs act as the leavening agent. Eggs contain a lot of moisture, and this turns to steam when it is heated, forming huge air pockets and a very puffy final products. Popovers are a spectacular example of this kind of bread.

Baking powder can get stale and lose its effectiveness. If

you suspect your baking powder is DOA, put a teaspoon in a cup of hot water. If it makes a big show of bubbles it's good, if not it's time for a new lot.

Some breads use no leaveners other than liquid, relying on the expansion of water turning into steam to create a little bit of rise. This is most common in flat breads.

Top four things to know about yeast

1. Dried yeast needs sugar and tepid liquid to activate it – leave it for 15 minutes to froth. To test the temperature of the liquid you can drop a bit on your wrist, you should not feel any heat or cold.

2. Instant or dried fast-action yeast (also called easy blend) is mixed straight into the flour.

3. Always store yeast in a cool dry place. If you have more than you are likely to use in a two-month period, freeze some of it.

4. Always check the expiry date before you use it.

Make your bread a meal

- Sweet breads love raisins, figs, currants, cranberries, apricots, fruit preserves and warm spices like cinnamon, ginger, allspice, mace, sugar glaze, fennel seeds.

- Savoury bread adores seeds, nuts, cheese, vegetables, olives, sun-dried tomatoes, herbs, caraway.

Three things bread doesn't need

1. Bread doesn't need water

Use whatever liquid you want (as long as it's something you would want to ingest). It is usually water, milk or egg, but you can try beer, stock, buttermilk, cream, potato water and puréed vegetables for colour and flavour. Milk gives a softer texture or crumb than water does. If a recipe calls for buttermilk and you don't have any you can either use a mixture of plain yoghurt and milk or put a tablespoon of cider vinegar into some milk and wait 10 minutes.

2. Bread doesn't need flour

Sprouts are one of nature's super foods. They are bursting with nutritional value, and they are really easy to grow. They can also be dried and ground, and then used to replace some or all of the flour in a bread recipe. Sprouted wheat berries will boost the bread's nutrients and flavour. Sprout for a much shorter period of time than you would for sprouts you use in a salad. The sprouts only need to be about 3 to 5mm long. At that point you have two choices as to how to proceed:

1. You can dry the sprouted wheat in the oven on a baking sheet at a very low temperature (or a dehydrator if you have one handy). Once totally arid, grind the sprouts into flour using a mortar and pestle or a clean coffee grinder. (You can freeze the flour in this form and save it for later.)

2. Use the sprouts in the same way as if you were adding raisins or nuts to a recipe.

If you choose option 2, only replace about 25 per cent of the flour with sprouted wheat if a recipe calls for just wheat flour.

3. Bread doesn't need dairy

In many quick breads, pancakes and biscuits you can replace the dairy and eggs with non-dairy and egg alternatives. Soya milk works as a substitute for regular milk in all cooking and baking. One egg can be replaced by:

- flaxseed slurry: 1 tablespoon ground flax seeds + 3 tablespoons water

- 50ml apple sauce

- 50g bananas, mashed

- 50ml silken tofu

- 50g dried plums, mashed

The four stages of making dough

Stage 1 Kneading

It can be an art form and doing it by hand takes patience. You can take out your frustrations by putting a serious hurt on your dough or you can passively throw it in a standing mixer and let the machine do the work.

Kneading by hand involves alternate pressing and stretching motions:

- Find a nice solid surface that won't move around.

- Put the dough in front of you and press down on it hard with the heel of your hand. You may have to put your body weight into it to really get it going.

- As the sides bulge out around your hand, pull them back onto the top so you have a ball again.

- Repeat.

About the time your arms feel they might fall off from exhaustion, test the dough. Try one of two methods: the windowpane test – take a small piece of dough and stretch it out, seeing if you can stretch it to the point it becomes translucent, without breaking it; poke the dough with your finger – it should spring back if the elasticity is right.

Some tips from Caroline

- Mixers are great for very wet doughs like brioche and ciabatta, which are near impossible to knead by hand because they are very messy and involve more of a lifting and throwing down motion. Always use the dough hook attachment, mix at a lower speed and check often with the windowpane test for doneness.

- You know you have over kneaded if the dough becomes very stringy and starts getting sticky. Over kneaded dough is broken dough and needs to be retired to the rubbish bin.

- Never knead dough (even very wet dough) with an electric beater using the beater attachment. It will do unholy things to the developing gluten and ruin the dough.

- Do not use a machine recipe for hand made or vice verse. The amounts and ratios do not interchange.

- Quick breads do not need the kneading and are at peace with all hand mixers.

Some tips from Lara

- During the earliest stages of the kneading process, if you have added too much liquid, you can balance it out by adding more flour. If you have not added enough liquid, you can just add more. You'll know when it's right because it won't stick to your hands but it won't crumble apart.

- Non-white flour will give more resistance then others when kneading bread. They will usually also require more liquid.

Stage 2 Rising

Different bread rises at different rates. Usually, but not always, whole wheat and whole grain breads rise more slowly.

- Lara's method: when you leave bread to rise, if you can't find a good place with no draught, leave it in a slightly warmed oven with the door closed. I like to leave mine on the shelf over the dryer, it's the warmest spot in the kitchen.

- Caroline's method: some doughs like to rise more slowly and need a cooler spot, even the fridge. If you want to slow the rising of your dough or leave it to rise overnight, the fridge might be a good place for it. If you want to stop it from rising altogether, yeast sleeps at temperatures below 4.5°C.

Some tips from Lara

- Cover the dough while it is rising. A clean kitchen towel works well, as does clingfilm that has been rubbed with a bit of oil. Alternatively you can spray the dough with some oil, which keeps it from sticking to the clingfilm if it rises all the way to the top of the bowl.

- Let the yeast do its job. No rushing. Bread that has not been allowed to rise properly will be dense and yeasty tasting. If it isn't rising at the rate you expected, just let it keep rising until it has gone as far as it will go.

- Skip this stage if you are making unleavened or quick breads.

Stage 3 Shaping

Always shape dough on a floured surface. Excess flour on the outside of the dough is seldom a problem.

- Rolls: roll the dough under your flat hand. Make them a uniform size for even baking.

- Boules: (a large round loaf, often called a farmer's bread) gently roll with the palms of both hands until in an even round shape.

- For small baguettes or batards: gently roll the dough into an oblong shape, flatten a bit then fold in half lengthways and press the seams together.

- For proper baguettes: shape as above and let it rest 5 minutes. Then gently pull the dough to the desired length. Press down, fold lengthways and press the seams closed.

Some tips from Caroline

- You don't need a tin to bake bread, be adventurous. You can make a loaf in a pot or pan that is ovenproof, you can have a round loaf on a baking sheet, a plaited loaf, rolls, flat breads or little breads baked in individual flower pots. Just remember to leave room for the bread to rise and you can make any size or shape you fancy.

- If you are baking on a sheet, flip the sheet upside down, it will trap some heat underneath and have a similar effect to using a baking stone.

- Go gently. After all that time the dough spent rising, try not to squeeze out all the air.

- Always seal any seams in a loaf by pinching them tightly together and put the dough seam-side down for proofing and baking.

Stage 4 Proofing

Most yeast breads, when finished rising, will get punched down, possibly left to rise again or shaped and left for a final rise called proofing. Be sure to cover the dough for this last stage.

Two cool things to do right before it goes in the oven

1. Score it: you can score or slash your dough before baking it. This makes it pretty and reduces the chance that seams will tear open during baking.

2. Wash it: an egg wash, applied to the top of dough with a brush will give the bread a shine and will help stuff stick to the surface. Seeds, seasoning or extra grains for decoration or flavour are a nice finish. A basic wash is an egg yolk, egg white or the entire egg beaten lightly with 1 or 2 table-spoons of water.

Some tips from Lara on baking

- Long-rising crusty yeast breads are made even crisper by steaming them in the oven. When the oven comes to temperature either put an old pan in the bottom and throw a few ice cubes in it or take a spray bottle of water and spray the oven with it. Close the oven door. Wait one minute, then put your bread in.

- Some quick breads, particularly corn bread, like to be cooked in a pan that has been heated to oven temperature before the dough is put in it. This gives it a nice crispy bottom.

- Tap the bottom of the bread to see if it's done – if it doesn't sound nice and hollow, put it back in the oven without its tin/sheet for a few more minutes.

- You can test a quick bread for doneness by sticking a knife into the centre and then removing it. If it comes out clean (no interior of the bread sticking to it) it is finished.

- If possible, remove the bread from the tin or whatever you are using as soon as it comes out of the oven or the steam will make it go soggy.

Cleaning up

When making bread, clean the bowl and/or worktop with a dry cotton cloth. Dry. Never clean it using a sponge with an abrasive surface because the gluten will stick to the sponge and ruin it.

When good bread goes bad

- It didn't rise: make sure you are kneading right – with force and for the right amount of time (5 to 10 minutes). Is the yeast out of date? Yeast becomes less effective over time. Maybe the water you used to activate the yeast was too hot and you killed it, or too cold and it didn't activate.

- It sank while baking: it most likely was left to rise for too long or was risen to quickly. You can still use that bread for breadcrumbs, if you aren't too annoyed with it to keep it.

- It burnt: umm ... perhaps you baked it too long. On the other hand, are you sure it is burnt? Very darkly browned burnt-looking breads are sometimes perfectly cooked.

- It is terribly dense: if it never rises to the point expected, it may have been under kneaded or it just needed more time to rise.

- While it baked it became wildly misshapen: could be a case of a split seam. If it is evenly cooked it will still taste good.

- It isn't as awesome as I thought it was going to be: with a yeast bread, maybe give it a second rise or try letting it rise a bit longer and at a cooler temperature. Maybe the recipe needs some massaging.

Some tips on storage

- White flours should be stored in an airtight container, in a cool dark place, but do not need to be kept in the refrigerator or freezer unless you are planning to keep them an exceptionally long time (over a year).

- Whole grain flours have the potential to turn rancid due to the natural oils in them. You can store them the same way as white flour, but it's best to keep them in plastic bags in your refrigerator or freezer. If you are worried it might be rancid just smell it – you'll know.

- If you are using frozen flour let it come to room temperature before you use it.

- If you are using frozen bread, let it defrost naturally, not in the microwave. Microwaves destroy bread.

- You can make crumbs out of leftover bread that's stale and freeze them. When it comes time to use them, you don't have to defrost them first.

- If you have a boule or country bread and have sliced it, store it cut-side down on a counter.

- Never bag hot crusty bread. It will steam itself soggy.

> ### *Bread is insanely old and insanely popular*
>
> There is evidence from archaeological digs, that bread flour was used as far back as 5000BC. Not only that, but it was widespread and has been found in many parts of the world including the Nile Valley, India, China and England too. Today, more wheat is grown worldwide than any other crop.

Eight great ways to use stale bread

1. French toast and bread pudding can be made from any bread that will absorb liquid and not fall apart: loaves, baguettes, croissants, quick breads.

2. Breadcrumbs can be made from the heels of loaves or any stale bread. Toast at 200°C/gas mark 6, then either crumble by hand or throw it into a blender or food processor.

3. Lightly dampen a day-old crusty loaf of bread, then pop in a hot oven for 10 minutes to soften.

4. Tortilla chips can be made by deep frying old corn tortillas that have been cut into quarters.

5. Panzanella is an Italian salad made from cucumbers, tomatoes, stale crusty bread and vinaigrette.

6. Crostini means little crust in Italian. Slice old crusty bread into 1cm-thick slices, toast or grill with olive oil and top with any number or things: tapenade, pesto, cheese, pâté, roasted vegetables.

7. Croutons can be made by either deep frying chunks of stale bread or by covering them in olive oil and spices and baking at 200°C/gas mark 6 until crispy.

8. Bread soups are made by adding old bread to a thin soup or broth and then either blending it or leaving it chunky. The best gazpachos are made this way. This method turns out a wonderfully thick and hearty soup.

Chapter ten

·

Pies

If you want to make an apple pie from scratch, you
must first create the universe.

DR CARL SAGAN, American astronomer (1934–96)

Pie making was such a mystery to me before I started the
one-year challenge. I thought it was something people
only did in the 1950s. Once I tried it I realised I loved
it. I loved everything about it. It was an odd time for my
family, because I started to make pies out of everything: too
many vegetables about to go bad – make a pie out of them;
leftovers from a couple of dinners – make a pie out of them;
jam – make a pie. Eventually the madness died down, but I
still love a good leftover-filled pie.

Pies are like snowflakes

There is no one pie; they come in all shapes and sizes:

- Beef Wellington: a very nice cut of beef usually topped with sautéed mushrooms or pâté is then wrapped entirely in pastry and baked. Sometimes one large one is made and cut up, sometimes small individual ones are made.

- Bottom crust, not top: this covers all tarts, and quiches. Often they involve blind baking (see page 182). They come in all sizes, and the flavours range from the traditional custard to summer fruit topped and on to the modern goat's cheese and red onion.

- Empanadas: these are wonderful Spanish and Mexican pies. The traditional Spanish ones are large, flat and served in slices. Mexican empanadas are generally smaller and similar to pasties or meat patties.

- Filo pies: Greek pies like spanikopita and and Middle Eastern desserts like baklava made with filo (also spelled phyllo) pastry. This is a fun, light and crispy pastry. Don't try to make it at home; buy some and experiment.

- Meat patties: a Caribbean treat. A small hand-held pie filled with meat (obviously), and it tends to be quite spicy too.

- Pasties: hand held, convenient and whether your favourite is the Cornish pasty or plain old potato, cheese and onion, there is a flavour out there for everyone. Many people say that to get the crust right you have to use lard but we've never found that to be true.

- Potato topped: fish pie or cottage pie, for example. If you are feeling fancy, you can use a piping bag to put the potatoes on the top, if not, then a spoon will do. A sprinkling of breadcrumbs adds a nice texture.

- Top and bottom crust: these are very traditional pies and range from game and pork to mince and fruit. These will not be blind baked (see page 182), and are usually made with shortcrust pastry. They are a wonderful pie to master because they are such a staple.

- Top crust, not bottom: another traditional method. Depending on the pub you go to, the steak-based pies tend to be served this way. As for making them at home, it means that all you have to do is roll out some puff pastry and slap it on top of whatever casserole you have going. It's as easy as . . . well, pie.

- Kulebiaka: Russian fish pie. The French call it coulibiac. Kind of like a fish version of beef Wellington. The fish (often salmon) is topped with rice, chopped hard-boiled eggs, herbs and spices (often dill). It is then wrapped completely in puff pastry and baked.

Varieties of pie crusts

SHORTCRUST/FLAKY PASTRY

Properties – A combination of firm, crisp, crumbly, flaky, buttery

Basic method – 2:1 flour to fat, with small amount of cold liquid to bind

Uses – Good for any kind of pie: sweet, savoury, shallow, deep. It's a go-to dough

Variations* – Cheese of all kinds, spice, herbs, ground nuts or alternative fats

SWEET SHORTCRUST

Properties – A combination of firm, crisp, crumbly, flaky, buttery, sweet

Basic method – 2:1 flour to fat, with slightly more cold liquid to bind. Sweetened with honey, syrup or sugar

Uses – Good with sweet pie filling

Variations* – Same things you might add to biscuits: warm spices, nuts, fruit zest, sweet cheese

PUFF PASTRY

Properties – Puffs up when baked, very light and flaky

Basic method – Many layers are achieved by chilling dough and butter, rolling it out, folding it, rolling it out and repeating 5 times

Uses – Turnovers, open pies with toppings (not fillings), canapés and desserts

Variations* – None

FILO

Properties – Greek pastry that is tissue-paper thin: crispy, light, papery when cooked

Basic method – Brush sheet by sheet with melted butter until desired number of layers are achieved

Uses – Good for anything sweet or savoury, turnovers, traditional pies, strudel

Variations* – None

BISCUIT-CRUMB BASE**

Properties – Sweet, crumbly, hard, buttery

Basic method – Mix bashed-up biscuits with butter; press into the bottom of a tin

Uses – For desserts: usually used for cheesecake

Variations* – Alternate fats, shredded coconut, ground nuts, sweet cheese

*Any of these variation ingredients should be very well chilled.

** Can only be used as a bottom crust.

Any type of flour can be used to make a pie crust, though heavier flours like wheat flour may require slightly more liquid to bind it and tend to be slightly more difficult to roll out. Still, a whole wheat pie crust goes very nicely with many of the savoury pies.

Three steps to making shortcrust pastry

1. Rub in the fat: make sure the fat is very cold and straight out of the fridge, and cut it up small before you start. Put two parts fat to one part flour in a bowl and rub together between your fingertips, lifting and letting them fall away. The lumps will get smaller and smaller till you have what looks like damp sand. You can do this using a pastry knife or a food processor to avoid melting the fat with your hands. For food processors, cut the fat into chunks and put it in a bowl with the flour. Leave it in the freezer for about 10 minutes, then dump into your food processor and blitz.

2. Bind it together: add a liquid, usually egg, water or milk. Try to keep the ingredients cool and do as little kneading or stretching as possible. Unlike making bread, you don't want gluten to develop. With that in mind, knead it just enough to bring it all together into a nice, smooth ball.

3. Let it rest: leave it in the fridge for about half an hour before using it. This allows it to relax and prevents shrinkage when baking. You can leave the dough in the fridge for more time, as long as you are using it in the next day or so. You can also freeze extra pastry, either in a well-wrapped ball or rolled out and lining a tin.

· A TIP FROM LARA ·

You can add flavours to pastry. Add any additional ingredients before the binding stage and use extra liquid if necessary. Herbs and spices add a nice touch, as do ground nuts.

In the 1800s it was a fairly common practice during large feasts, to decorate a fowl pie by topping it with an actual stuffed bird. The 1890 edition of Mrs Beeton's cookery book has an illustration of a game pie with a stuffed pheasant on top. It was also common practice to make the pie in the shape of the animal that was in the pie.

Six steps to making a pie

- Step 1: roll it out. Always roll pastry away from you rather then back and forth, to avoid battering it.

- Step 2: once you've rolled the dough to the right size, gently fold it in half, in order to lift it into the tin. For some variety, try using something other then a regular pie tin:
  - springform cake tins make lovely tall pies
  - muffin tins will make wonderful small individual pies
  - small ovenproof bowls are great for dinner pies
  - at a pinch you could use a loaf tin or even a pan as long as it is ovenproof.

- Step 3: fill it.

- Step 4: seal the lid by pinching it together round the edge with your fingers, or use a fork to press the edges together.

- Step 5: if you want to decorate the pie, any leftover dough can be cut into shapes and stuck onto the top with water. Brush the top with egg wash for a pretty finish.

- Step 6: poke steam holes into the top so the crust doesn't go horribly soggy or, even worse, burst.

· A TIP FROM CAROLINE ·

If you are having trouble rolling the dough put it between two sheets of clingfilm. If it's far too soft to deal with, chill it in the fridge first then roll it out in between two sheets of clingfilm.

Avoid these pitfalls

- Too much flour will make the dough too crumbly.

- Too much butter will make it difficult to roll.

- Too much liquid will leave it tough.

No pie please, we're British

In 1657 Oliver Cromwell banned people from eating mince pies. The ban was not lifted until the Restoration in 1660.

Flying blind

Blind baking means to pre-cook the pastry case without the filling. This prevents bubbling, warping, over browning, puffing, cooking unevenly and makes the crust crisp. It's especially good for non-cook or quick-cook fillings. Blind baking a pie shell can be done well in advance; you can cool the shell and store it in an airtight container. And it's dead easy to do.

- Prick the base with a fork and cover it with foil or grease-proof paper.

- Fill the bottom with baking beans (or dry beans or rice).

- Bake at 190°C/gas mark 5 for 15 minutes.

- Remove the beans and paper and bake for another 5 to 10 minutes till golden.

After blind baking if there are holes or damaged bits, stick on scraps of raw dough while it's still hot – the heat will stick them together.

A pre-baked pie crust can provide you with a super-quick lunch or dessert. You can fill it with crème fraîche, smoked salmon, rocket and capers or, if you want a super-fast sweet pie, try sweetened cream cheese with fruit on top.

No pie please, we're American

In the American state of Kansas, it used to be against the law to serve ice cream on cherry pie.

Some tips from Lara on fillings

- If you are using fruit for the pie and it is very tart, slice it more thinly or into smaller chunks so it can absorb sugar more easily.

- Pies are a great way to use up leftovers. I like to use a spring-form cake tin and make layers of leftovers in my pies. Try rice, diced vegetables, cubed bits of leftover meat, hard-boiled eggs, anything you have around.

- You can add some breadcrumbs to the bottom of a savoury pie to absorb extra moisture and keep the crust from going soggy. Bits of cooked pasta or rice will also work.

- Adding gravy to a leftover pie keeps the filling quite moist. Make a tall pie and put the gravy in close to the top. Not at the very top because it will make the top crust soggy, but high enough that it won't leak all the way down making the bottom crust soggy.

What to do with leftover pastry

Shortcrust pastry scraps can be brushed with a little butter, and sprinkled with cinnamon and sugar or with grated cheese and baked as a special treat. Extras of any type of pastry are quite fun to play around with. Just wrap something in it and throw it in the oven, see what happens. Try leftovers, fruit, jam, vegetables, cheese.

Not to start a culture war, but ...

'As American as apple pie' and 'as British as apple pie' are both phrases that are widely used.

How to make humble pie

Though now it is just an expression, it was originally a real pie. The name comes from the French *numble* or *nomble* meaning deer innards. When originally conceived, this pie was presented as a special treat to the hunter who had killed the deer, but by the seventeenth century it had evolved into a different sort of thing. It became a pie that was made out of all of the parts of the animal the wealthy would not eat. The humble pie, or umble pie as it was known, was fed to the servants. That's why now we use the expression 'eating humble pie' to mean that we are being taken down a notch.

Take whatever bits of the animal (usually deer, maybe cow) you have leftover: heart, liver, kidneys, intestine, tripe, feet, brain, sweetbreads. Put into a pie along with: apples, currants, sugar, spices and egg custard (savoury, not sweet).

Chapter eleven

·

Eggs

A hen is only an egg's way of making another egg.

SAMUEL BUTLER, English novelist (1835–1902)

The egg is cross-culturally a symbol or metaphor for the universe. And why not? It hosts, then hatches life. The yolk not only looks like the sun, but is one of the few food sources of vitamin D, which otherwise can only be synthesised in your body from direct sunlight on your skin. It can also almost single-handedly make a whole array of delicious, nutritious meals. With eggs in the house, you'll never be stuck for something to eat. Does anything else do the same trick?

Why fresh eggs don't float

Every egg has a small pocket of air in its larger end. As the egg ages, the protein of the egg white is absorbed into the yolk, thinning the white. Eggs lose moisture and carbon dioxide through the shell, replacing it with more air inside the shell. Thus this handy way of testing the egg for freshness: drop the egg into a glass of water. If it sinks and lies flat it is fresh; if it stands on its point, it's a little older, but still fine; if it floats, it's bad – gently, gently get it out of the house!

The white of the egg will also be slightly more solid when the egg is fresher. If you crack a fresh egg onto a plate, you will see that the white looks like a platform, holding the yolk up high. If you do the same with a less fresh egg, it will look like a yolk swimming in the white.

· A TIP FROM LARA ·

You can freeze egg whites, just make sure you label how many are in the bag or container. You can't count them once they're combined. If you do forget to label them, an average egg white weighs about 40g.

A fresh egg has a more pronounced chalazae – the white cord-like strands at either end of the yolk. Any blood flecks in an egg do not mean that it is fertilised and do not effect the flavour, but if you are superstitious it may mean bad luck – much like a double yolk, which means death to a family member and no yolk, which means all around bad news.

The colour of an egg's yolk, to some degree, depends on the hen's diet. The shade can range from pale to bright yellow. Barley or wheat feeds produce a pale egg yolk and though the flavour is not affected people like a deep yellow yolk, leading many farmers to add marigold petals to the feed (artificial colour enhancers are not allowed). The colour of the shell is a result of the breed of the chicken.

> ### When the power goes out
>
> In some parts of the world without refrigeration people grease eggs to hold off the spoiling process. Greasing them seals many of their almost 17,000 pores, preventing moisture loss.

Three ways to be a good egg

1. Be cool: always refrigerate. The supermarkets may not do it, but it's important for you to.

2. Don't overstay your welcome: try not to keep them for more than one week in the fridge and heed the use-by/sell-by date. It should be stamped on each individual egg, in addition to the carton they came in. If your eggs are out of date but you suspect they might still have some life left to them, use our handy egg test (see above).

3. Straighten up: eggs should be stored large end up in the carton they came in to prevent them from absorbing any weird flavours or odours from strongly-smelling food neighbours.

> ### Impeccable timing
>
> Hens left to lay eggs and nest with them in their natural setting will lay 1 or 2 eggs a day until they have about 15 to 20 eggs. Even though the eggs were laid over a 10 to 14-day time period, the chicks all hatch on the same day.

Twelve must-have egg recipes or a dozen for your dozen

1. Basted and fried

To fry an egg, heat a pan to medium high, add some fat, crack an egg in it and either flip the egg once the whites harden or leave it yolk-side up. Basted eggs are cooked in the same way as fried eggs, but are cooked in the side of the pan facing away from you so you can baste them with hot fat, be it butter, oil or animal fat. They are insanely good. Here's what to do:

- Melt 75–110g of fat (butter is best) in a sauté or heavy-bottomed frying pan. Start, as you would to cook fried eggs, over medium heat.

- When the whites start to turn opaque, start gently pouring spoonfuls of the fat over the egg. Baste until the top of the yolk starts to turn white for a very soft yolk or until the top of the yolk looks completely white, if you like them more well done.

- Serve these in your fry-up instead of plain fried eggs. They are excellent with grilled crusty bread and fresh parsley fried in the remaining butter.

2. Baked, shirred or en cocotte

The eggs are baked for a short period in individual containers in which they are served. You can include cooked shredded meat or potatoes on the bottom, cheese or herbs on the top, or line the sides of the container with a rasher of bacon. En cocotte are eggs baked in cream.

- Preheat the oven to 200°C/gas mark 6. Grease a small container, add meat or potatoes if you choose and then crack an egg into it. Add any toppings.

- Cook for about 10 minutes, longer if you've added meat and cheese, less for a runny yolk.

- Serve with asparagus spears or toast soldiers.

3. Benedict

More of a preparation than a cooking method.

- First make some hollandaise sauce (see page 35).

- Toast some muffins while you poach the eggs and fry some ham.

- Put the ham on the muffin, the egg on the ham and cover with hollandaise. If you don't have a muffin a toasted crumpet or plain old piece of toast will do.

- Serve garnished with a sprig of fresh herbs or with a slice of melon or some asparagus.

Variations include:

- Blackstone: with bacon and tomato instead of ham.

- Florentine: with sautéed or creamed spinach instead of ham, and mornay sauce (see page 36) instead of hollandaise.

- Hussard: substitute a mushroom and red wine sauce for hollandaise.

- MAD: served with curry sauce – ham or bacon optional – and topped with diced spring onions.

- Sardou: this Cajun version consists of a large steamed artichoke heart topped with a poached egg, hollandaise sauce, anchovies, truffles and ham.

4. Eggs in a basket or boat or hole or popeyes

These are eggs fried in slices of bread that have a circle cut out of the centre.

- Get a piece of good-quality bread and cut a hole in the centre of about 3 to 4cm across. You can use a biscuit cutter or a small glass.

- Heat a frying pan to medium-high, add some fat, put the bread in the pan for about 30 seconds, flip it over and wait 15 seconds.

- Crack an egg into the hole. Wait for egg to harden a bit then flip the whole thing again.

- Season and serve either on its own (it is toast and egg all in one), or as part of a larger fry-up.

- As a nice variation, put some roasted red pepper slices over the egg as it goes into the pan.

5. Devilled eggs

A cocktail party favourite because you can eat them with one hand, present them with a variety of fillings and decorate them in creative ways.

- Hard boil a few eggs, let them cool and shell them.

- Cut them in half lengthwise, leave the whites intact and remove the yolks.

- Mash the yolks with some mayonnaise, mustard and salt and pepper.

- Fill the whites with the yolk mixture using a spoon, a piping bag or a freezer bag with the end cut off.

- Sprinkle with paprika and serve as part of a larger picnic or buffet table.

- As a nice variation, try adding one or some of the following: finely chopped: chives, onions, spring onions, Jalapeno peppers, cornichons, celery or olives, white wine vinegar, hot sauce, sugar (just a touch).

6. Tortilla – Spanish omelette or frittata

This is the Spanish and Italian version of an omelette. It can have any number of fillings – good choices are potatoes, mushrooms, onion, ham, cheese and herbs. They are a great way to use up scraps of cooked meat and vegetables. Cooking with heat from the bottom and the top allows the tortilla to puff up a bit and gives it a beautiful texture.

- If the filling requires cooking, start with that (for example, sautéing onions, browning mushrooms, heating up some diced meat).

- Pour in the beaten and seasoned eggs and cook until the bottom and sides are firm but the centre is still a little wobbly. This can take between 5 and 10 minutes for a large frittata.

- Remove from the hob and put the pan under a preheated grill. The omelette is done when the eggs are set, which will probably take up to, but not more than 5 minutes.

- Serve sliced hot or cold with some good crusty bread and a green salad.

7. Scrambled

The French way: slow and low with butter and cream.

- Whisk 3 eggs.

- In a saucepan melt 15g butter over low heat or in a double boiler.

- Add the eggs, whisking constantly until they just start to hold together, then remove from the heat.

- Keep stirring for another 3 minutes while adding 15ml double cream. Season and serve with toast or as part of a fry-up.

- As a nice variation, try any of the fillings for omelettes listed below.

8. Omelettes

If you get a few people together who have firm but conflicting views on how a proper omelette is made, they could debate the subject all day or until a fight breaks out. A French omelette is runny, hardly brown, if at all, and should take no more than a minute to cook. Other omelettes are completely cooked by heading from burner to grill and spending a final minute there to puff up. Some are stuffed, some are left plain. One can even debate whether a plain omelette is an omelette at all. Why isn't it just scrambled eggs? Here is a general method for omelette making.

- Whisk together 3 eggs.

- Put a well-seasoned frying pan or non-stick frying pan with sloping sides over high heat and add some fat. We suggest butter.

- Pour in the eggs and cook without stirring for 10 to 15 seconds. Then, keeping the pan over the heat, move it in circles to swirl the eggs round gently, tilting the pan back and forth to get them cooking evenly.

- Add any filling (about 50–100g) to one half of the egg circle.

- When the eggs are cooked enough gently fold one half over the other.

- At this point you can either put the frying pan under a grill for about 30 seconds to get it to puff up, varnish it with some butter on top, or serve as is either on its own on a garnished plate or with chips or green salad.

Good omelette fillings: mascarpone and jam; chopped tomatoes, dill and cream cheese; leftover ratatouille or other roasted vegetables; sausage, Cheddar, potatoes; green peppers, ham, Swiss cheese; spinach and feta; asparagus, ham and Parmesan; chorizo and peppers; sautéed mushrooms with thyme.

9. Poached

If you are poaching, use the freshest eggs possible. The stronger white holds its shape better during cooking. You can also poach eggs in oil, effectively deep frying them.

- Bring a saucepanful of water plus 60ml white vinegar to a boil; then turn down to a simmer.

- Crack the eggs one by one into a cup and gently slide them into the water. Cook, covered, for 3 to 4 minutes.

- Remove them with a slotted spoon and drain well. Serve hot or cold. You can refrigerate them in cold water if you want to use them later in salads or sandwiches.

- You can also poach eggs in wine for added flavour, or add to a simmering soup.

- Serve as part of eggs Benedict, on warm salads, in soups, or just with toast.

10. Scotch eggs

These days we so often see those mini versions of Scotch eggs with a little bit of chopped egg in the middle. Real Scotch eggs are huge and fun and so easy to make, you'll want to have them all the time.

- You'll need 75–150g of sausage meat for each hard-boiled egg. With floured hands, flatten the sausage meat into a round patty and wrap the egg in it.

- Dip the Scotch egg into some beaten egg and roll it in breadcrumbs.

- Heat enough oil to cover the eggs to 180°C. Fry two or three at a time for 6 to 8 minutes. Make sure the oil isn't too hot or they will burn before they are done cooking. Drain on paper towels.

- Serve hot or cold on their own or as part of a larger picnic or buffet.

> Always check the label when you are buying sausage meat. Some brands contain as little as 50 per cent meat. Buy one that has about 80 per cent if you can.

11. Strata

This is an eggy brunch casserole that is part bread pudding, part quiche. They take 2 days to make. The first day you build it, then leave it in the fridge overnight giving the eggs and bread time to meld. It is a great dish to make for breakfast if you have guests. No prep in the morning, just 45 minutes of baking. This recipe serves 4.

- You need 1.25 kilos of ripped crusty bread gently mixed with 350–450g of any fillings or seasoning you would like: sautéed, roasted or mashed vegetables, cheese, fruit, sausage, ham, bacon, maple syrup, honey, for example.

- Butter a soufflé dish or ovenproof saucepan and put the bread and fillings in it.

- Beat 8 eggs and combine them with 350ml of milk. Add any seasoning you might want: vanilla, salt, pepper, cayenne pepper, rosemary, thyme, cinnamon, nutmeg.

- Pour the egg mixture over the bread. Put it in the fridge overnight or for at least 8 hours.

- Cook, covered at 180°C/gas mark 4 for 45 minutes, until it is puffy and turns a golden brown.

- Serve on its own on a garnished plate. Depending on what's in the strata it is nice served with whipped cream, maple syrup, salsa, roasted red pepper sauce.

12. Hard boiled (grrrrrr ...)

If you are hard-boiling you ideally want a slightly older (though not bad, obviously) egg. The flavour will still be just as good, and the fact that the white has slightly receded from the shell makes the egg much easier to peel.

- Put a few eggs into a saucepan of cold water. Turn the heat to high and bring the water to a rolling boil. Count to 30, then remove the pan from the heat, cover and let it sit for 12 minutes.

- Remove the eggs from the pan and run cold water over them. Doing it this way, the eggs are less likely to end up cracked, or overcooked with a grey ring round the yolk. For soft boiled remove the eggs from the hot water after 4 minutes and shock them in an ice bath for a couple minutes, not so long as to cool them, but long enough to stop them cooking.

- Tea eggs are hard-boiled eggs that have had their shells slightly cracked (without peeling them) and then are boiled again in dark tea, soy sauce and or spices.

- You can also slightly crack a hard-boiled egg and leave it overnight in a cup of water with a teaspoon of food colouring added. It won't be as tasty as a tea egg, but it will be really pretty.

- Serve in sandwiches or with salads or even just on their own as a quick snack.

Lovely flavour combinations

Anchovies, artichoke, asparagus, avocado, basil, beans, black pudding, bread of all kinds, bubble and squeak, butter, caviar, cheese, chives, coriander, crab, cream, dill, duck fat, garlic, hollandaise, hot sauce (like Tabasco), meat of all kinds (bacon!), miso, mushrooms, olive oil, olives, onion, oysters, pancakes of all kinds, parsley, polenta, potatoes, prawns, salmon (smoked or not), salt and pepper, sausages, soy sauce, spinach, spring onions, toast, tomatoes (raw or fried), Worcestershire sauce.

> The second Friday in October is world egg day.

Know your source

If you buy eggs from supermarkets they offer several different kinds, it's important to know where they got them from and how the chickens are kept.

- Free range means the chickens have been allowed to run around outdoors, and organic means that the land on which they were raised is up to organic standards, as well as being a guarantee that there was no non-medicinal use of antibiotics in their feed. Many are fed a vegetarian diet.

- Barn-raised chickens, though not allowed out of doors, are still afforded the extra comfort of being raised in an open barn. This isn't necessarily as good as it sounds. Often the hens are crammed in shoulder to shoulder in overcrowded barns, and have no room to move. Many of these barns practise de-beaking (which is just what it sounds like). It's painful for the chicken, and some scientists and farmers say it continues to be painful long after the healing process, but it is considered necessary to keep the chickens from pecking at and killing each other in their overly tight quarters.

- Battery-farmed chickens are often de-beaked, they are al- ways kept in a tiny cage and never given the chance to stand up or move around. They are likely to have been fed non- medicinal antibiotics to try prevent illness in their unhygienic conditions. Many are fed the remains of culled chickens.

Egg world records

- An ostrich egg is 21 times the weight of a hen's egg with an average weight of 1½ kilos. The largest egg of any living bird – they're so strong, you can stand on them.

- The bee hummingbird lays the smallest eggs at ½g. You could fit 4,500 bee hummingbird eggs into on ostrich egg.

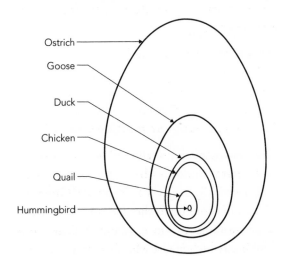

- The greatest number of recorded yolks in one egg was 9.

- It takes about 2 kilos of feed for a chicken to produce a dozen eggs.

An acquired taste

A balut is a duck egg that has a nearly completely developed chick inside. It is boiled, then eaten shell and all. Mmmm . . .

Tale of the century

The century egg, or thousand-year egg, is a duck egg preserved by being buried in a mixture of lime and charcoal for three months. This process changes the egg from white to a deep brownish colour and creates a cheese flavour. In Hong Kong it is a popular street food, prepared much like Scotch eggs but coated in fish mash instead of sausage.

Four reasons to keep the eggshell

1. They can be composted.

2. Ground eggshells are sometimes added to foods as a way of adding calcium.

3. Gardeners sometimes use crushed eggshells round their plants to keep slugs and other crawling pests away.

4. The ancient Romans used to crush eggshells on their plates, believing that they would prevent evil spirits from hiding there.

Cook your way through history: the California gold rush

Hangtown Fry

Hangtown fry got its name from the town where it was invented and has the dubious honour of being California's first standard dish. It was a meal of the privileged who had been lucky enough to strike gold in California in 1849. It's a fry-up of what were the three most expensive ingredients in Hangtown at the time: oysters, eggs and bacon. This serves one hungry miner.

    2 slices of bacon
    2 eggs
    6 oysters

In a heavy bottomed frying pan, fry the bacon. Remove from the pan. Fry the oysters in the bacon fat. Cut up the bacon and return it to the pan. Pour the eggs over the oysters and bacon and scramble until they are done. Serve hot with a few shots of whisky.

Chapter twelve

·

Cheese and Yoghurt

A cheese may disappoint. It may be dull, it may be naive, it may be over sophisticated. Yet it remains, cheese, milk's leap toward immortality.

CLIFTON FADIMAN, American author (1904–1999)

Cheese is just aged milk and cow stomach

Cheese-making surely started by accident. Before we had sports bottles and thermoses, people lugged liquids around in animal stomachs, bladders and intestines. They are elastic, hold water and are resilient. Some people still use them today. Rennet, the enzyme that makes milk solidify, is found in the stomach of cows. So it seems likely that the inventor of cheese stored milk in a goat's or cow's stomach and upon finding the results ate it either out of bravery or sheer hunger and liked it!

Top five things to look for in a cheese shop

1. Look for a shop where they cut the cheese to order, instead of having pre-wrapped chunks lying around.

2. See if you can taste a cheese before you buy it. You should be encouraged to.

3. Find a shop that is at least fairly busy. It's important the stock turns over quickly so you aren't buying old leftovers.

4. If you need a certain kind of cheese, or if you like a particular type and want to try something similar, they should be able to help you out. Sometimes you'll come across a recipe that calls for an unusual cheese. If you can't find the one you are looking for, it helps to know the general families of cheeses when picking a suitable substitute. A good cheese shop should be able to point you in the right direction.

5. Make sure the shop display is clean and well laid out. The care put into the display indicates they'll care about their cheese in general.

Some cheese is fake

Processed cheese – which isn't really cheese, but more an oil-based pressed and dyed food product, is the most consumed category of cheese in the United States. One of those cheeses is called Easy Cheese and comes packaged in a spray can, much like canned whipped cream.

Some tips on serving and storage

- Firm cheese can be wrapped in plastic and kept in the fridge. If you are storing them for a while, it wouldn't hurt to change the plastic every couple of days.

- Stinky cheese can be wrapped in parchment paper and then wrapped in plastic wrap over that, or you can put your paper-wrapped cheeses in a plastic container with the lid slightly ajar in your fridge.

- Keep blue cheese separate from other cheese because the mould can travel.

- Fresh cheese should be kept in the container it was sold in and eaten soon after purchasing.

- Feta and fresh mozzarella should be stored covered in brine or water. Changing the water every couple of days helps extend their shelf life.

- Most cheese should be served at room temperature. Seldom if ever does cheese go bad if left out overnight, making it a favourite high-calorie food for campers. Some cheese can stay unrefrigerated for days before going bad. If you like a rich or pungent hard cheese, leave it out. It will sweat and may dry on the outside, but will be good until it goes mouldy.

Cool contraption – the cheese apartment

Is a neat little storage device that you can buy. They are typically small boxes, slightly reminiscent of a cage, as the sides are made of meshed metal, allowing air to flow freely through and keep the cheese at room temperature without exposing it to anything undesirable. It is mainly for cheeses with a rind or which are waxed.

Some cheese is against the law

Casu marzu or rotten cheese is widely found in Sardinia although it is illegal. Maggots are introduced to the cheese to further the fermentation process into one of decomposition. The maggots can be cleared out before eating the cheese or not (some people consider the maggots to be a delicacy). The maggots can also jump up to a height of 15cm if they are disturbed!

Portion calculator

Pre-dinner hors d'oeuvres 110–175g per person

Cocktail party hors d'oeuvres 150–175g per person

Composed cheese plate 50–75g per person along with bread and other garnish

If you are just sitting with a knife and a block of cheese . . . run with it.

The perfect cheese platter

Consider colour as well as flavour, and make sure you have some flavour enhancers (like fruits and jams or olives and cornichons) and palate cleansers (such as toasted hazelnuts, smoked almonds, or roasted cashews). Take the cheese out of the fridge a few hours before serving. Brie and Camembert should come out 8 hours early. Fresh cheese should be kept covered in the refrigerator till it's time to serve them. A good complement to the cheese would be a platter of pâté and charcuterie.

The equipment

- That big wooden cutting board you use for kneading dough and chopping is perfect. Giving it a good rub down with mineral oil will clean it up nicely.

- Something to cut or spread with. It's best to have a different knife for each cheese. There are knives specifically for cheese platters and some designed for specific cheeses.

The cheese

- Pick three to five cheeses. Six or more if you are having a really large party, spread over two platters.

- The cheeses should contrast in flavour: tangy + sweet + creamy + bold.

- And in texture: hard and gritty + spreadable + soft with a rind + semi-hard.

Bread and biscuits

- Get more than you think you will need. They run out fast. Have a variety of crackers, some sweet, some savoury. Avoid cheese-flavoured ones. A hearty and thinly sliced raisin nut bread is always welcome.

- Here are some other ideas: dense fig cake, herbed or pepper crackers, water crackers, Melba toasts, crostini, sliced fruit and nut bars, baguettes.

Lovely flavour combinations

Apples and pears (thinly sliced or julienned), apricots (dried), blackberries, cherries (dried or fresh), dates, figs, grapes, honey, honeydew melon, nuts in honey, peaches (sliced), pecans (candied or spiced), pineapples, preserves (apple, pear, fig, apricot), quince paste, raspberries, strawberries.

Some cheese is scary

Many people believe that if you eat cheese right before you go to sleep, it will give you nightmares. They call them cheese dreams.

Easy Peasy Cheese Fondue

clove of garlic, peeled
350ml of white wine or champagne
450g in total of up to three cheeses, grated –
Emmental and Gruyère are the classic choices
3 tablespoons kirsch or vodka

Rub the inside of the saucepan you are using with the garlic, add the wine and bring to a simmer then add the cheese and let it melt. Add the kirsch or vodka and stir. Simmer for 5 minutes then transfer over a small flame and serve with crusty bread, apple chunks, boiled new potatoes.

Cheese families

I often find myself looking for a specific type of cheese for a recipe. If I can't find it, and I'm not familiar with it, it can leave me a bit confused about what to use as a substitute. If you have that trouble too, then these lists might help.

Soft with unwashed rind

- Brie
- Camembert

Blue cheeses

Some of these will be much softer, some much harder, but they are all in the blue family.

- Dolcelatte
- Gorgonzola
- Roquefort
- Saga
- Saint Agur
- Stilton
- Shropshire Blue*

*This one is a red cheese, so it looks very different, but if the colour doesn't spoil the presentation of your dish, it will make a fine substitute.

Cheeses with holes

These cheeses all have holes – and similar flavours.

- Emmental
- Gruyère
- Havarti
- Jarlsberg

Hard gritty

These hard cheeses are good for grating and sprinkling

- Grana Padano
- Parmesan
- Romano

Soft fresh cheese

- Mascarpone

- Ricotta

Semi-hard

The flavours of these cheeses will vary quite a bit, but they will all give your dish a bit of a bite, as well as melting quite well. They will produce different results, but can be used in place of each other, to some degree of success.

- Cheddar

- Comté

- Gouda

- Edam

- Lancashire

- Manchego

- Provolone

- Raclette

- Red Leicester

How to Make Yoghurt

~

Yoghurt is easy to make. A culture is added to milk and a controlled curdling takes place. You can skip the yoghurt maker. You need a thermometer, whole milk and a small amount of plain, live yoghurt which contains live bacteria to act as the starter.

  1 litre of full fat milk
  3 tablespoons plain live yoghurt

Bring the milk to a boil in a heavy-bottomed pan, stirring constantly. Then let it cool to about 50ºC. Add the yoghurt and stir well. Transfer to a bowl, cover with cheesecloth and set in a warm place between 30 and 45ºC. If you have a gas stove stand it over a pilot light or wrap the bowl in a towel to help it keep warm. Leave it for about 15 hours then transfer it to the fridge. If the yoghurt is thinner than you would like, line a colander with cheesecloth and drain it until it reaches desired consistency.

Chapter thirteen

·

Sweet Things

One of the reasons making cakes is satisfying is that
the effort required is so much less then the gratitude
conferred.

NIGELLA LAWSON

Sweet foods more then any other area of cooking seem to
be very culture specific, from French pastries to Indian
galub jamin, from Greek baklava to the good old Victoria sponge. The one thing that remains constant is that we love
them. They represent the pinnacle of comfort cooking and
eating. Every culture has their version of cakes, biscuits and ice
creams in addition to their more regionally specific dessert
choices. Learning to make them yourself is a wonderfully
worthwhile use of your time and many are easier to make than
you might think. They will be better for you, will taste better
and will never fail to impress. Over the course of the year-long

challenge, I found my favourite chocolate cake, my favourite bread pudding, the best and easiest Victoria sponge ever, and a new level of comfort with my comfort foods.

Some sweet terms

- Creaming: when butter and sugar are beaten together until the sugar granules dissolve. Keep beating until the mixture is light and fluffy-looking.

- Folding: this is not about strength but about delicacy. You need to combine ingredients while retaining as much air as possible. Use a metal spoon or rubber spatula, something with a thin edge. Just use your wrist and scoop, turn the bowl, scoop, turn, scoop, turn until the mixture is fully combined.

- Ganache: an all-purpose chocolate mixture, made with one part chocolate and one part cream, milk or soya milk. Used for the centre of truffles or the cream centre of sandwich biscuits.

- Hard peak stage: like when making meringue when the whisked peaks of egg white should stand tall.

- Imitation extracts: vanilla for example. To be avoided – the flavour will ruin anything unfortunate enough to come into contact with it.

- Parchment paper/baking paper: your new best friend. Use it to line baking sheets instead of greasing them so they stay clean and your food doesn't stick to them.

- Piping bags: usually used to make icing into decorative shapes which depend on the shape of the nozzle you use.

They can also be used for dough and fillings. If you don't have one you can use a freezer bag with the corner cut off achieving the same, although likely slightly less artful results.

- Soft peak stage: whisking egg whites or cream until they form a soft peak that falls back down.

- Tamis: an Indian flat, drum-like sieve that comes in handy when making fruit sauces and curds.

Cake basics

Most cakes are a combination of fat, sugar, eggs and flour. There are versions of cakes that omit one or more of these ingredients, but for the vast majority of cakes, those are your building blocks and the differences in texture and form come down to how you combine them.

- Cakes made with whisked eggs, like angel food cake are light and airy, and usually have little fat. The texture comes from whisking the eggs into either soft or hard peak stage, and then folding them into the cake batter.

- Cakes made with creamed butter and sugar, like Victoria sponge, have a high fat content and therefore a less delicate texture but usually a more buttery taste. Eggs, flour and flavourings are added to the creamed butter and sugar. When making cakes that use the creaming method, make sure to add the beaten eggs one at a time and thoroughly mix in each one before adding the next. Also, don't over mix after adding the flour; if you do, the flour begins to develop gluten, which is what makes bread chewy but not what you want in a cake.

- Cakes made by melting the ingredients are the richest and densest kind. Some of these are flourless, taking their shape from whisked eggs or other ingredients that hold their shape when cooled.

Cakes are a bit temperamental. You may find they come out slightly differently each time you make them, but they are not unreasonable and there are some things you can do to make the process easier.

Some tips from Lara

- Make sure all the ingredients are at room temperature before you start, unless the recipe states otherwise.

- Preheat the oven completely before you put anything in it.

- Don't open the oven unless you absolutely have to. It changes the temperature and can damage the cake, especially if it is a delicate one. Besides, nobody likes people peeking while they are getting ready.

- If you use a tin that is a different size or shape to the one the recipe calls for, the cooking time will most likely change. If you are taking a major detour from the recommended size, it would be best to use a very basic recipe like a Victoria sponge.

Three things that make a cake fall

1. Low oven temperature: if you regularly have trouble with cakes falling, get yourself an oven thermometer. Many ovens can vary by 10° in either direction from the temperature on the dial.

2. Measuring incorrectly: changing or mis-measuring the amount of fat and sugar in a recipe can easily make a cake fall, as well as making it less delicious.

3. Out-of-date baking powder: baking powder will lose its effectiveness over time. Check its use by date.

A Fool-proof Sponge Recipe

Known as quarte-quarte or four quarters. So named because the cake is made by using four ingredients in equal parts. Weigh four eggs (in their shells). Whatever the weight was, that's how much flour, sugar and butter you are going to use. Equal parts, all ingredients.

> 4 eggs
> equal weights of butter, sugar, self-raising flour
> 1 teaspoon vanilla extract
> pinch salt

Preheat the oven to 180°C/gas mark 4.

Cream the butter and sugar till it's fluffy, add the eggs one at a time, then the vanilla, then sift in the flour with a pinch of salt. Fold together. If the mixture needs loosening, add a few spoons of milk. Divide between two 20cm sandwich tins and cook for 25 to 30 minutes. Cool on a rack and fill as you would normally, using cream, lemon or lime curd or icing.

Some tips from Caroline

- If you are cooking using a water bath with a springform cake tin, it's a good idea to wrap the outside of the tin with a couple of layers of kitchen foil to make sure the water doesn't get in.

- For many cakes you can test if they're done by inserting a toothpick or knife in the centre, then pulling it out to see if it's clean. Some cakes cannot be tested this way because they will have moist centres or they may need to set while cooling. Check each individual recipe to be sure.

- Most cakes benefit from being removed from their tins and cooled on a wire rack soon after baking. Rich fruitcakes do not. Let them cool completely before you attempt to get them out of the tin, otherwise they are likely to break.

Biscuits are awesome

Unlike cakes, the method of making biscuits doesn't necessarily dictate the finished product. There is no quintessential creamed or moulded biscuit. A chocolate-chip biscuit, for instance, can be made by almost any of the methods below. Still, understanding each technique means that no biscuit recipe will take you by surprise.

Methods of mixing

- Creaming: start by creaming together the butter and sugar, then add whatever other ingredients the recipe calls for. They firm up as they cool.

- All in one: the ingredients get added together, then stirred to combine, super fast, super easy. Just make sure the butter is soft or your arm will fall off from the mixing.

- Refrigerating: no baking involved, just melt, mix and chill. They tend to be chocolate heavy.

- Melting: another melt and mix, but these are mixed with flour and baked.

- Whisking: these are light because they use stiffly whisked egg whites, like meringues. Usually that means that little fat (if any) is needed.

Methods of shaping

- Rolling out: for biscuits with very firm doughs. A rolling pin is the best utensil, then they're shaped using a cutter.

- Moulding: for dough that is too soft to roll with a pin, but firm enough to roll into a ball with your hands.

- Piping: with a piping bag – they tend to be very decorative, and quite firm when done.

- Tray bakes: brownies, flapjacks and shortbread. Cooked all in one tray, then cut into pieces. Great for parties, and very easy to transport.

Some tips from Lara

- Many tray bakes set as they cool. Don't think you have to cook them until they're fully set; you'll just burn them. If they are going to set hard (many of them do), it's a good idea to cut them halfway through the cooling process, otherwise they may shatter or crumble when you try to slice them.

- Biscuits made with baking powder tend to be soft. Ones that don't include any baking powder tend to be crisp.

- Biscuits, like anyone else, do not like to be crowded. Air needs to circulate round them, so don't overcrowd the baking sheet, and if you are using more then one sheet, make sure the oven racks are about 20cm apart.

- Turn the baking sheets part way through for evenness of browning. If your oven has hot spots, and if you are cooking two sheets at once, check them both, one may cook faster than the other.

- Watch very closely in the final few minutes, biscuits can go from under- to overdone in the blink of an eye.

- Remove biscuits to a rack immediately after you take them out of the oven unless they need to set, otherwise the bottoms will continue to cook and may burn. As they cool they release steam and if they are still on the tray the steam will get trapped and they'll get soggy.

Four ways to dress up biscuits

1. Use an interestingly shaped biscuit cutter.

2. Before you bake them, decorate the biscuits with nuts, cherries or jam.

3. After cooking and cooling, decorate with icing, candies, sprinkles or melted chocolate.

4. Sandwich them together using icing or ice cream.

When good biscuits go bad

- Too tough: overworked dough, or too much flour.

- Spread too much during cooking: too much butter or sugar, or over beaten.

- Cake-like: too much flour or oven too hot.

Three simple icings

1. Butter icing: great for covering cakes and fairy cakes: cream together 100g butter and 100–150g icing sugar. Keep beating and adding more sugar until you get the consistency you like. Then just add a flavour or a colour, for example 1 tablespoon of cocoa powder.

2. Cream cheese icing: slightly more tang than butter icing. Use a 2:1 ratio of icing sugar to cream cheese. Bring the cream cheese to room temperature and beat it until it's smooth, then slowly beat in the icing sugar. Add in a flavouring such as citrus juice, vanilla or almond.

3. Decorative icing: great for drizzling over biscuits and fairy cakes. Mix icing sugar with a liquid (milk, lemon or other citrus juice, etc.). Add a little liquid at a time and keep mixing until it is thin enough to drizzle. You can also make it slightly thicker, so you can spread it.

Ice cream

Ice cream is sexy

In Japan, there is an ice cream flavoured with deadly pit viper. It's considered an aphrodisiac. Other weird Japanese flavours include ox tongue, eel and whale.

Dead Easy Ice Cream

MAKES ABOUT 1 LITRE
175g sugar
100ml milk
450ml double or whipping cream (or yoghurt if you
want to make frozen yoghurt)
2 large eggs
225–325g of anything else you feel like adding

In a saucepan combine the sugar, milk and cream, put it on a
high heat and keep stirring until bubbles form at the edge.
Turn down the heat. Meanwhile whisk the eggs in a bowl.
Add half the cream mixture to the eggs, stir well, then add the
eggs to the rest of the cream in the saucepan and, over a
medium heat, stir constantly until the mixture coats the back
of a metal spoon. Add anything else you want at this point,
excluding nuts and chocolate chunks. Let the mixture cool in
the fridge for a few hours then pour it into an ice-cream
maker. Now add chocolate chips or nuts and follow the ice-
cream maker's instructions.

To make a chocolate-based ice cream add 110g cocoa
powder to the milk and cream mixture at the beginning.

Lovely flavour combinations

Chocolate and chillies; carrot and cardamom; Greek yoghurt,
lavender and honey; avocado and lime; Guinness and brownies (with optional walnuts).

Ice cream is gross

Traditional ice cream is made with cream, sugar and a flavouring, sometimes egg too. Some cheap supermarket versions are made of milk and vegetable oil, but some truly ghastly ones are made with chicken fat, so beware if you are a vegetarian. Or even if you're not.

If you don't have an ice-cream maker

Semifreddo is a creamy frozen dessert. It's also Italian, which automatically makes it more sexy. You can make it any flavour with any additional treats, just as you would with ice cream. Liqueurs go nicely in semifreddo.

SERVES 6
3 eggs, separated
110g caster sugar
350ml double cream
110–300g of any flavouring you choose. The lesser amount for liqueurs or fruit purées, more for nuts, chocolate chunks and chopped fruit

Line a loaf pan or a mould with clingfilm. Beat the egg yolks with the caster sugar until they turn pale yellow. Beat the egg whites until they come to stiff peaks. Whisk the cream to peaks. Add the flavourings to the egg yolks. Gently fold the egg yolks into the whipped cream and then the egg whites. Pour into the mould, cover with clingfilm and freeze overnight.

To serve, remove from the mould and slice just like you would a loaf of bread

---

Who needs a freezer?

The first frozen deserts were made in the middle of the Persian desert in 400BC. Getting ice and keeping it was quite a production. Labourers would haul it from mountain tops during the cold season, then would keep it in giant underground caves, called *yakchals*, to preserve it into the summer.

Feel the fear and do it anyway – part 1

Fried Ice Cream

A wild, seemingly impossible mixture of hot and cold. Different combinations of things are fun to experiment with. Sugar, cinnamon or other seasonings are nice too.

    1 pint of any ice cream you choose
    1–2 eggs, beaten
    125–225g biscuit, cereal flakes, ground nuts or panko,
       crushed very fine
    sunflower oil

Roll out balls of ice cream, no larger than a golf ball and return to the freezer for an hour. Then roll the ice cream balls in the beaten egg and dredge them with the crumbs. Return to the freezer for another hour. Heat 6cm oil to 180–200°C.

Take the ice cream out of the freezer. Fry the ice-cream balls for from 30 seconds to a minute, drain and serve as soon as you can get them onto a plate with whipped cream, fruit coulis or caramel sauce.

Ice cream is rich

On the menu at Serpendipity 3, a dessert restaurant in New York City, is a $1,000 ice-cream concoction called the golden opulence sundae. It is sprinkled with gold leaf and eaten with a golden spoon.

Mouth-watering Meringues and Pretty Pavlovas

These are the perfect things to make when you have lots of leftover egg whites if you've been making mayonnaise, hollandaise, curds or custards. Make sure the whites are at room temperature before you start. The bowl should be totally grease free and dry. (This also means no yolk at all, as yolks are fat.) Any fat or grease will prevent the eggs whites from reaching the right consistency.

egg whites (3 eggs serves 3–4 people)
60g sugar for each egg

flavourings: vanilla or almond extract, citrus zest,
  crushed nuts, saffron, cinnamon, cardamom, cocoa
  powder (1 tablespoon per egg white), or espresso
  flavour (1 teaspoon per egg white).

Preheat the oven to 180°C/gas mark 4.

Whisk the egg whites in a large bowl. You'll know they are done when they form stiff peaks and you can hold the bowl upside down without the eggs falling out. Slowly add the sugar a spoonful at a time. Fully incorporate each spoonful before adding the next. Once all the sugar is in, whisk again until the meringue is really shiny. This could take as long as 7 or 8 minutes. To test if it's ready, dip in a finger and rub a little between your finger and thumb, it should feel perfectly smooth, not at all grainy. If you are adding a flavour, gently fold it in.

Use a spoon to drop the meringues on to a baking sheet that has been lined with baking paper, and then use the back of the spoon to make peaks in your round biscuits. You can also use a piping bag. For a pavlova, make a larger shape with a flatter top. Put the meringue in the oven and after 5 minutes turn it down to 120°C/gas mark ½ , then bake for 1 to 1¼ hours depending on the size of the meringue.

Pavlovas make people angry

Australia and New Zealand have been in a 70-year battle over who gets the bragging rights to claim themselves to be the home country of the pavlova.

· A TIP FROM LARA ·

- For meringues to be crispy on the outside, chewy on the inside, do not over cook them or they'll dry out. If you are not feeling confident, or if you are making a large pavlova, you could also add cornflour and vinegar, which helps keep the centres soft. You need about a teaspoon of cornflour per 2–3 egg whites and about half that much vinegar. If you want them crispy all the way through, increase the cooking time.

- Serve pavlovas as soon after assembling as possible. Meringue absorbs all liquids and will get soggy.

Meringues have feelings too

You may get some bubbly outcroppings of sugar on your meringues. This is called sugar weeping.

If this happens while it is cooking, it could mean the sugar wasn't added gradually enough or that the oven was too hot. If it happens as they're cooling, then they weren't cooked long enough.

Honey is good for you

Some people believe that eating locally produced honey will help to lessen the effects of hay fever.

Chocolate

Caroline's chocolate primer

Cocoa farmers harvest the cocoa beans, shell them and leave them to ferment, usually on the ground near where they are grown. During fermentation – which is the beginning stages of rotting – they are raked, turned over and left in the sun to mellow the flavour. Then they are dried on large outdoor racks, roasted in a similar manner to coffee beans, ground down into powder and shipped to chocolate makers who mix the powder with oils or fats, sugar and vanilla. They then sell the chocolate to chocolatiers who make confections like chocolate bars, sweets and truffles.

Two foolproof methods for melting chocolate

- Put it in a bowl over a pan of simmering water. The bowl shouldn't touch the water.

- Put it in a bowl in the microwave and heat it in 30-second increments.

Some tips from Lara

- For best results, cook with at least 70 per cent cocoa solids, unless stated otherwise. Some people say anything over 55 per cent is acceptable but 70 per cent is so easy to find these days, there's no real reason to skimp.

- If you are melting chocolate and it 'seizes', becomes hard and unworkable, stir in a few drops of vegetable oil to loosen it up.

Blood and chocolate

Chocolate syrup was used for blood in the famous 45-second shower scene in Alfred Hitchcock's movie, *Psycho*, which actually took seven days to shoot.

Four cool things to do with melted chocolate

1. Dip fruit in it: it's quick, easy and wonderful. Dry the fruit before you start, then dip it in the melted chocolate and leave it to cool on greaseproof paper. Strawberries are the classic choice, but any fruit works. Try using dried apricots or segments of satsuma.

2. Make a shell: any hollow container can be a chocolate mould (espresso cups, petit four cases . . .) Pour the melted chocolate in, swirl it round, pour it back out and wait for the residue to cool and set. Repeat. Use more layers the bigger the mould is (so it doesn't collapse). Fill it with whatever you want.

2. Make a sauce: 100ml liquid (water, milk, cream, spices, vanilla, butter, rum, whisky, cognac, fruit liqueur or fruit juice) per 200g chocolate. Heat the liquid, then add the chocolate broken into pieces off the heat and leave it till it melts, then mix till smooth.

2. Decorate with it: you can make designs by drawing with melted chocolate from a piping bag onto greaseproof paper. Once the chocolate has cooled and hardened, peel the paper off. You can also shave chocolate with a vegetable peeler or a zester for a quick decoration.

Lovely flavour combinations

Bananas, berries, caramel, cherries, chilli peppers, citrus zest, coconut, coffee, Earl Grey tea, figs (fresh), fruits (dried), ginger, lemon, liqueurs, mint, nuts, peanut butter, red wine, salt, vanilla, verbena.

Some fun with fruit

If you are faced with a bunch of bananas getting ripe and no foreseeable way of eating them all, frozen bananas dipped in chocolate then rolled in chopped nuts, shredded coconut, granola or sprinkles will take care of the problem for you.

Super Simple Custard

We all love custard over just about any dessert, but so few of us feel confident about making it. Everyone I know, though, who tries it for the first time says the same thing: 'Oh, that was easy!' You'll say it too.

    300ml single cream or a 1:1 mixture of double cream
       and milk
    1 teaspoon vanilla extract
    3 egg yolks
    1½ tablespoons sugar, caster is best, but granulated
       works too
    1 teaspoon cornflour (optional, for a thicker custard)

In a saucepan heat the cream and vanilla just to boiling point. Take it off the heat and let it cool for a couple of minutes. Meanwhile, whisk the yolks with the sugar (and cornflour if using) until it's pale. Add a tiny bit of the slightly cooled cream to the egg mixture and whisk it in well. Continue adding the cream a little at a time, whisking constantly. Once it is all combined, pour it into a clean saucepan, and heat it gently, stirring or whisking the whole time, until it has thickened (not more then 5 to 10 minutes; if you're using cornflour, it only takes a couple of minutes). When it's done, it should be thick enough to coat the back of a wooden spoon. Take it off the heat, and whisk it quickly to cool it down.

If it starts to look lumpy

- Take it off the heat and whisk as hard as you can.

- Pour it into another clean pan.

- Submerge the bottom of the pan into cold water; keep whisking.

Then continue cooking till done. Strain before serving to get out any mini-lumps.

Some tips from Lara

- To use a vanilla pod instead of extract, just open it up and scrape the seeds into the cream before heating. After taking the saucepan off the heat, allow it to infuse till the cream has cooled down, then strain it to remove the seeds and reheat.

- You can also use vanilla sugar in place of ordinary sugar and vanilla extract.

- If you are not using the custard right away then either stir it frequently as it cools or cover the top with a circle of wet greaseproof paper to avoid a skin forming.

- To reheat custard put it in a double boiler or in a bowl set over a pan of simmering water to avoid curdling.

Feel the fear and do it anyway – part 2

Flambé

Here is how to impress and terrify your friends with your enthusiasm for intentionally causing a huge burst of flame in your house.

- Slice some fruit. Classics are bananas, mangoes, and pineapples. You can sauté them in butter first, grill, marinate, season as you please.

- Put them into a shallow sauté pan with sloping sides. That isn't to say you can't do this in a cast-iron griddle pan, but it is more elegant and easier to get the dramatic effect you are going for. Don't use non-stick.

- Pick your flammable material. Rum is a popular choice, but anything 80 per cent+ proof should work. Do not try to flambé with wine, port or sherry. You will fail miserably which is especially tragic when you are trying to be flamboyant.

- Cook 75–175ml of the chosen liquid with the fruit and some sugar over a medium-low heat until the sugar has dissolved. Remove the fruit to a serving dish. Stand well back as you light the liquid in the pan with a match and then pour the flaming syrup over the fruit.

How to Make Barley Sugars

Barley sugars are a traditional boiled sweet. For a long time they had a reputation for being beneficial to your health because they were made with barley water, but these days they are generally made just with sugar and no barley at all. Part of their claim to fame was that they were the favourite sweets of Alice Liddell, who was the girl *Alice in Wonderland* and *Alice Through the Looking Glass* were based on and written for. The sweet shop in Oxford where Alice Liddell bought her barley sugars is still there today, though now it is a gift shop called Alice's Shop selling *Alice in Wonderland* merchandise.

110g pearl barley
900ml water
450g sugar
a pinch of cream of tartar
juice of ½ to 1 small lemon

Put the barley in a saucepan with the water and simmer for a couple of hours. Remove it from the heat and let it settle completely. Take off 225ml of the clear water from the top of the pan. Pour it into a clean pan with the sugar and cream of tartar. Heat slowly, stirring until the sugar melts, then continue heating without stirring until the syrup reaches the hard crack stage at a temperature of 150–155°C. It should be a light brown colour, and if you drop a bit into a glass of cold water, it should form hard threads that crack when you bend them. Remove from heat and allow to cool for a minute, and then add lemon juice.

Pour the barley sugar onto a heatproof greased board, tin or plate and, as the mixture starts to cool (it will be far too hot to touch when you first pour it out, you will burn yourself severely if you try), very, very carefully cut it into long strips, and twist them around. Then leave to harden completely. Alternatively, you could pour it directly into well-greased moulds designed for the purpose and let it harden before turning them out.

Chapter fourteen

·

Where to Go from Here

Cooking is a constant learning process. There are always more tips, techniques, ideas, interesting trivia and fantastic theories to discover. This book was an attempt to collect some of the most important things we learnt but we're always on the lookout for more. So, we hope, will you. Here is a list of further resources for you to continue your own cooking adventure.

Our blog

Cooking up a Storm is found at cookbad.blogspot.com. It is the inspiration for this book and tells the entire tale of how we learnt to cook. Many things from *Fresh Eggs Don't Float* are covered in depth there (with recipes!!), as well as all sorts of great and interesting stuff that didn't make it into these pages.

Lara's favourite cookery books

Any cookery book will have at least one good recipe in it, but these ten are the ones I trust entirely. I have never had a bad cooking experience from any of them.

Bell, Annie, *The Country Cook*, London: Collins and Brown Ltd, 2007
Many of the recipes are traditional but prepared with an unusual twist or made with fine ingredients and caring preparation so they are unbelievably delicious. Try her oxtail cottage pie which is worth the price of the book alone.

Blashford-Snell, Victoria and Snow, Selina, *Favourite Recipes from Books for Cooks:* 1, 2 and 3, Kent: Pryor Publications, 2001
Book For Cooks is a book shop in London selling nothing but cookery and cooking-related books. They also have an experimental kitchen where their chefs try out recipes from the books and perfect their own recipes for books such as this. Annie Bell was one of their chefs. The book has loads of helpful information, like telling you what can be done in advance and how to store and reheat the dishes. It is helpful and informative and the food rocks! It was their chicken braised in balsamic vinegar with porcini mushrooms and sundried cherries that won my heart for ever.

Child, Julia, *Mastering the Art of French Cooking, vol. 1*, New York: Alfred A. Knopf Inc., 2000
A classic. Julia Child is the chef who introduced French cooking to Americans, and this book is exactly that, an introduction. For most things she starts with a basic recipe that is

in itself is a lovely meal and then follows with variations to suit different tastes. Her daube de boeuf á la provençale, a variation of a beef casserole, is out of this world.

Clark, Sam and Sam, *Moro East*, London: Ebury Press, 2007
Written by two wonderful chefs who were inspired by their allotment, this book is full of recipes that were made from the produce they grew or from meals fellow allotment owners shared with them. It is Middle Eastern food that is fresh and flavourful, ranging from simple salads to elaborate five-part dishes. Their mansaf (a meatball soup with a saffron broth) is a big family favourite.

Dunlop, Fuchsia, *Revolutionary Chinese Cookbook*, London: Ebury Press, 2006
When I lived in New York, my favourite Chinese food was bean curd in black bean sauce. I ate it all the time. Since moving to the UK, I have been looking all over to try to find it again. This book finally delivered it to me, under the name Peng's home-style bean curd. It, along with everything else I have tried from this book, makes me very happy.

Goodman, Myra, *Food to Live By: The Earthbound Farm Organic Cookbook*, New York: Workman Publishing Company, 2006
This book includes one of my favourite dishes ever: maple-brined pork chops. If I could only make pork chops one way for the rest of my life, this would be it. This is another book of classic food, but better than you remember them. The focus is obviously on organic food, but whether you choose to go organic or not, these recipes are amazing.

Hom, Ken, *Ken Hom Cooks Thai*, London: Headline, 2001
Ken Hom really opened up Asian cooking for me. I would
recommend you try any of his books, but I chose this one
because of his recipe for spicy tuna salad. The last time I made
it for someone, they immediately went out and bought the
book on the strength of this one recipe alone.

Lawson, Nigella, *How to be a Domestic Goddess*, London:
Chatto and Windus, 2003
I love Nigella's books, not just for her recipes but for the way
she writes. This one was the first of hers I owned and it's still
my favourite. There are some savoury recipes that are very
good, but for me this book is all about the desserts. She is a
wonderful cake maker and with this book, I became one too.

Oliver, Jamie, any of his books
Jamie is heroic. I also love his food. When I started cooking,
preparing his recipes gave me a lot of confidence. I was never
sure how things were going to come out, but after trying more
and more of his dishes, I began to trust that I could produce
food that was better then I had hoped. I have tried recipes
from all his books and have never been disappointed. He has
a recipe for a bread stuffed with cheese, hard-boiled eggs and
Parma ham that I have made more times then I can count,
and every time it has received rave reviews.

Saleh, Nada, *New Flavours of the Lebanese Table*, London:
Ebury Press, 2007
When I first got this book I loved it so much I made dinner
from it every night for over a week. Everything I made was
delicious. I was worried at first that my boys wouldn't be on

board, but it turns out they loved all of it. They asked for the pumpkin dip (similar to hummus) from this book months later – and that's a long time to a two- and a four-year-old.

Caroline's favourite books about food

Bourdain, Anthony, *A Cook's Tour*, London: Bloomsbury, 2002
This guy is my imaginary drinking buddy. Not a cookery book, nor reference, but a tale of a man travelling the world in search of the perfect meal. One of my favourite reads of all time and totally inspirational. I swear it will make you plan your next vacation around food.

Doherty, Gail and Sher, Lacey, *Down to Earth Cookbook*, San Francisco: Pollinator Press, 2007
The best book I've ever read on cooking meat- and dairy-free food. I highly recommend it to anyone who is interested in experimenting with vegan cuisine. It offers a number of recipes that will appeal to both strict vegans and people who might just want to have a healthier and more food-conscious diet. This is a book that I couldn't stop cooking from after I got a hold of it.

McGee, Harold, *McGee on Food and Cooking: An Encyclopedia of Kitchen Science, History and Culture*, London: Hodder and Stoughton, 2004
This is the definitive book on food knowledge as far as I am concerned. Anything and everything you need to (or not) know is in there.

Montagne, Prosper, *Larousse Gastronomique: The World's Greatest Cookery Encyclopedia*, London: Hamlyn.
Originally published in French – but hardly exclusive to French cuisine, it was translated into English 30 years ago. It is an excellent read providing amusing tangents that are strange and inadvertently hilarious. The first edition that I have is great for the bizarre factor, while the more recent editions are terrific for extreme food knowledge.

Pepin, Jacques, *Jacques Pepin's Complete Techniques*, New York: Black Dog and Levanthal, 2003
When he says complete techniques, he means it. Want to learn how to make a sugar sculpture to house your dessert? Maybe you need to make those fancy paper booties to fit over the drumsticks of your next chicken? It's all in there. Every technique has excellent step-by-step instructions along with photos.

Reinhart, Peter, *Crust and Crumb: Master Formulas for Serious Bread Bakers*, Berkeley: Ten Speed Press, 2006
Reinhart woke up one day and decided that his purpose in the world was to teach people how to make the best bread possible. It is a somewhat academic read, but you will come away with a more solid grasp on bread theory than you thought possible. Most importantly, you'll learn how to make the Holy Grail of baking . . . a perfect baguette.

Sahni, Julie, *Classic Indian Cookery*, London: Grub Street, 2004
By far the best place to start learning Indian cooking. She lays out all aspects of Indian meals in an elegant prose that reads like a novel. Best of all she gives menu suggestions which are

incredibly helpful when venturing into a new type of cuisine. When I first got this book I cooked nothing but the recipes from it for a month. It is the perfect gateway to international cooking because it primes you to cook in a way that isn't standard to Western sensibilities. A very horizon-broadening book.

Waters, Alice, any of her books but particularly *Chez Panisse Vegetables*, New York: HarperCollins, 2003
She is a big advocate of buying seasonally and locally. She not only lovingly tells you how to cook it, but if it comes from the ground, she'll give you tips on growing it too.

Caroline's favourites online

When I first started this project I had very few cookery books. Instead, I started with my best friend, Google. Anything I wanted to know I would google. I cannot express in words my love for the Internet and all the wonders it has to offer. If, at two in the morning you must find a recipe for oatmeal raisin biscuit dough ice cream, the Internet is there for you.

Buying stuff

I try not to buy ingredients online, not because what I have bought has been sub-par or I fear my credit card number will end up in devious hands, but because such a large part of the fun for me is tracking down an exotic item, scoring it and running home to make a long-planned recipe. But I have had the advantage of living in culturally diverse urban areas where, if you look hard enough, you are almost certain to find it. If you are unable find something that has no ready substitute, the Internet is the place to go. Google it and a purveyor will appear. If all else fails, you can find almost everything on eBay. Food included.

Knowing stuff

www.nutritiondata.com is the best website I've found if you are health conscious and want to know exactly what it is you are putting into your body. It is laid out in easy to understand graphics and contains clear and concise content.

www.lovefoodhatewaste.com will tell you how to store food, gives detailed portion calculators, has leftover guides and everything you need to know about stretching what you've got in the fridge and not wasting a bit of it.

www.cheftalk.com calls itself a food lover's link to professional chefs. It has a terrific forum for chatting with chefs, caterers and those who aspire to be, with advice, inspiration or general hand holding.

www.foodsubs.com is a cook's thesaurus, the 'encyclopedia that covers thousands of ingredients and kitchen tools'. I have found it utterly indispensable.

www.epicurious.com has a comprehensive and very user-friendly recipe collection with user reviews and a detailed search engine to help you zero in on any dish you might want to try. It includes a number of specifics from ingredients and techniques to diet restrictions and wine pairings. For example, if I have a huge amount of asparagus in the fridge that I must use within the next 24 hours and need some inspiration, I usually head over to epicurious for a nice new way to prepare it.

Sharing stuff

Discussion boards on cooking abound on the Internet. My favourite is chowhound.com. If you are looking for something – from the best tequila in your price range to where to pick up some fresh curry leaves – people on chowhound will know. It also has a wealth of interesting useable recipes. People can get pretty spicy with their opinions on this board – which I like. So join up (free!), jump in and be spicy too.

Over the past few years a number of food social networking sites have popped up. Think myspace for gastronomes. My personal favourite of these is opensourcefood.com. It is easy to navigate, beautiful and populated with very good cooks making quite interesting dishes.

Foodbuzz.com is a cute one, populated with content by food bloggers, including us. You can search for cooks in your area, look for recipes by ingredient. If you are a blogger, this is a nice place to beef up your community.

So ... go! In the invaluable words of Jacques Pepin, 'Finally, cook, cook, cook, cook, and cook again!'

Index